T0196618

SCREAM WITHOUT RAISING YOUR VOICE

One Pastor's Journey

Jody Scott Jones

WESTBOW
PRESS®
A DIVISION OF THOMAS NELSON
& ZONDERVAN

CONTENTS

INTRODUCTION

Writing a book has always been something on my to-do list. But, as we will soon discover and discuss, if you stay with me, you'll see that I sort of have a problem getting from thought to action, but I feel that God has brought me to this point, whether it be for a final book or for a therapeutic purpose. But to reference a *Star Wars* meme, "The resistance is strong with this one." I've done almost everything I could possibly do to resist the start. Even as I type, I can't bring myself to finish listening to Arlo Guthrie's "Alice's Restaurant." I have picked the longest song I know; it's eighteen minutes long, edging out "Free Bird," by Lynyrd Skynyrd, by a full nine minutes. I've committed in my mind that it's a generator of creative juices. We'll see.

In 2012, a family in our community lost a son to a swimming accident. Over Labor Day weekend, the boy and some friends were at a lake, and it was the first night of the weekend. It was the last jump from the dock, the last light of the day, and the last time he would be alive. Without a life jacket, he jumped from the top of the dock house into the water, and something went wrong. He never came up on his own. Devastation. Trauma.

Trauma mastery is when someone or a family acknowledges the trauma in their lives and does what they can to stop it from happening again or happening to other people. It's a way of dealing with the trauma, to give it some meaning, to give purpose and value to the life lost, or the damage incurred, or the pain suffered, or all of the above. This is what the family of the drowning victim has done. They've started an organization called LV Project, which brings awareness to anyone and everyone they can through 5Ks, donations, sponsorships, radio spots, web pages, legislative impact, and whatever else they can do to give meaning to this horrific event. In some ways, *Scream without Raising Your Voice* represents my trauma mastery. In many ways, I found myself drowning and in need of help, but through the grace of God and the help of others I have surfaced, although not without water in my lungs and some brain damage. But I am alive, and this is my story.

For more information on the LV Project, go to www. theLVProject.org.

PART I

PAST

CHAPTER 1

REMEMBERING

"Let's start at the beginning." This is a comment I often make to my clients. Then I ask, "How far back can you go? What do you remember?" I'm not good at it myself, so sometimes I feel bad for asking. Most of my memories are actually falsely generated or established from photographs. I "remember" going to Disneyland because of the pictures of me and my brothers. I "remember" the vinyl couch because of the picture of me and an unnamed friend playing underneath it with my head out and his head in, making it look that I was folded in half, tying my own shoe. I "remember" our first pet because of the pictures of the snow in the backyard and Captain, the German shepherd–collie mix, snuggled in his doghouse. Oh, and I "remember" that it used to snow a lot in Texas—because of the pictures. But maybe that's how it works for many of us. I don't know if I can really say I didn't remember outright; I just know I remember better when I have visual aids. Sometimes remembering is a blessing, but sometimes it can be painful.

I'm the youngest of three boys; we are each about two and a half years apart. And my earliest true memories come from my grade school days. I have lots of memories from that time, but I'm always impressed when people say they have toddler—or even infant—memories. Why is this important? Why are our memories worth discussing? Why does this story start here? Because our memories help us identify our stories—your story, my story—and that's what *Scream without Raising Your Voice* is about. Stories. I've spent a good amount of time over the last several years being impacted by the stories of others, and now, through what feels like God's timing, it's time for me to write. Maybe for therapy, maybe for impact, maybe for some purpose yet to be known, but the prompting is to write, not to figure things out. In the ministry, it seems we are figuring out that it's the stories of people's lives that make the most impact. It's why Jesus spoke in parables—why he told stories.

One of the things I enjoyed doing most in my life was writing and acting in church dramas. It was a season in Western church life that has come and gone, as we read research that tells us millennials are tired of being entertained that way. Apparently, this next generation of Christ followers wants liturgical services, solid foundations, and processes to which they can be connected. I think it's a shame that the church drama has gone by the wayside. Stories are powerful. Let me clarify. I think it's a shame that *quality* church dramas have gone by the wayside. I have never in my life seen people more moved by a church service than when they connect to a drama and see their lives being played out on the stage. It opens their hearts, and as if scales are falling off their eyes, they see their lives in a new way. Stories are like that. I hope this story is like that for you.

My story starts way back before I remember, back before I existed, according to Jeremiah 1:5, Ephesians 2:10, and several other truths in the Bible; however, grade school is my first real memory. You should know that to protect the men and women in my story, names will be changed, and through the help of others in my life, additional stories will be added to muddy the accountability but strengthen the point. Let's get a little more background. I remember giving my life to Christ when I was eleven, in June of 1980. There were no pictures of the event, but it was written in the front of my Bible. So that helped. Lucky me. Or maybe there were pictures. I just never saw them in the big box of pictures my parents kept in the bottom drawer of the 1970s built-in desk in the family room. They were kept there during most, if not all, of my childhood, as far as I can remember. Want to look at the pictures? Bottom drawer. I think they are still there, according to the last random comment at the monthly family dinner.

I don't remember the salvation prayer or the process, but it was written in my Bible, so it must have happened, right? I guess that's sort of like the purpose of today's Instagram. If you didn't take a picture, it must not have happened. But what I do remember outright is that it was an act of obedience. Not an act of obedience to God, but as I was the youngest of three, it was my time. "Do you want to give your life to Christ?" Uh, sure. Obedience. I was obedient by nature, so this fit the theme. Ask, do, perform, achieve. And then what happened later that week sealed the memory. I'm not sure if it was a Wednesday night or a Sunday night (let's go with Sunday night), but I was baptized right in front of the whopping crowd of Sunday night attendees. I found my way through the back rooms, stairs, awkward robes, and ill-locking doors to the little pool of water behind the pulpit. The pathway to the baptismal is always a mystical place for kids to explore during the week or after church, but then it turns into the hall of terror when you actually use it in the proper way. I assume when they baptize and they say "in the likeness of His death," they pretty much mean when an eleven-year-old has to walk down a creepy shag-carpeted hallway, poorly lit with a single-socket incandescent bulb, to the executioner—er, I mean pastor—waiting at the other end of the journey. Why do I picture a medieval town circle with all eyes on the victim being brought to the platform about to lose his head? The excitement, the fear, the expectation to overcome death and walk in newness of life! They could not have designed a better analogy for the process of being baptized. It was finished. I survived. I was a follower of Christ. Maybe you can relate?

I believe that seeds of our later fruit are planted early and often since we know God has designed us from before we were created and because our works are planned before we are in existence.

> For we are his workmanship, created in Christ Jesus
> unto good works, which God hath before ordained
> that we should walk in them. (Ephesians 2:10)

Everything matters. Everything is a part of His plan. The trouble is that we often seem to be about one thought behind His purpose for us. And that's if we're lucky. More than likely, we are a season or a lifetime behind Him. It's usually 20/20 hindsight vision that gives us the clearest perspective, and even though we know that, we still long for full-frontal knowledge. My story is about connecting dots, seeing patterns, and trusting God—from good to bad to good again with lots of good and bad bounces along the way. It's a story of redemption and a story of the unwavering goodness of God and the journey that may provide hope to others. At one level, it's about First World problems. At another, it's about the deepest recesses of humanity. It would later become an issue, but that day I performed a simple act of obedience. It didn't mean I didn't love God; it just meant that my obedience was likely more out of a need of worldly acceptance and approval than a deep love for my Creator. I did what I felt was expected so I would be accepted. This is the concept of expectance of acceptance.

Speaking of the deepest recesses of humanity, when I was a teenager, I worked in a furniture store. It wasn't a busy one but was one where people buy something significant about once a day, maybe even once a week—lots of lookers, a few buyers, and lots of downtime. It gave me spending money through college, and it allowed me to be on display and to be held captive so my future wife would know where to find me. But beyond that, the only thing that really sticks out is a memory I can't seem to shake—one of those memories that will stay with you a lifetime. There was a certain couple who came in and walked around the place, not regularly, just once that I recall. They didn't look to be overly interested, but they were shoppers nonetheless. After a short look around and some chitchat, one of them asked me if I would ever consider studying the Word of God for a living. I said no. They obliged my rejection, and life went on. Mind you, this was more than thirty years ago, but I can't seem to get it out of my head. And of course, the more I refer to it, the more it settles into my amygdala (I hope to use more brain words later). The teenage mind is not real receptive to those kinds of random solicitations, but a seed of some sort was planted within me. As an adult with 20/20 hindsight vision, I often think of that couple who came into my life much like Old Testament prophets. Or maybe they were spiritual farmers. Regardless, the words haunted me, in a good way, over the years, becoming one more stepping-stone in my story.

Narrative therapy is about finding a theme in your life and identifying, hopefully, the person God has made you to be and what His plan is for you. It often takes the mind of a trained outside observer to help you see clearly; however, with some practice and awareness, I believe the self can be someone's best ally in this journey as only you truly know your hidden thoughts, fears, and motivations. What drives you? What seems to be a recurring thought in your internal dialogue? How far back can you go with your memories? They matter. They shape you and the course of your life. It's why therapy works. It's why God's plan for life, relationships, and self-care are important. It's why everything we experience matters. We are tough, resilient, fragile machines designed in His image to work best in His will. Think about this for a minute. Do you think that your life is made up of several important moments and that the rest of it is "filler," things you do while waiting on a God moment? In the video world, they call this the B roll. It's just the stuff to put in the background and take up time until we get to the important stuff. Or do you acknowledge that everything is designed by and guided by God through our free will and His desire for us? I agree that it hurts your brain if you think about minute-by-minute orchestration and our free will playing in tandem, and if you think that somehow sovereignly works, but I think we can agree that our lives are not full of filler B roll. God is fully aware of what is going on, and He has a plan for you. He's planting seeds, arranging meetings, creating circumstances, and giving you opportunities to grow into who He wants you to be. All these things become themes in our lives, best discussed by searching our memories.

As a sidenote, it may be important to get your memories verified if you have doubts. I won't get into a philosophical discussion about how reality is only defined by our memories or what actually happened, but I will tell you that for most of my life I was pretty sure that we, as kids, at some time, owned a spider monkey in some way, shape, or form. I don't have any pictures, but for some reason that memory is in my head. I was wrong. Psychology would call that a *false memory*. So would common logic if you are one of my family members. So those kinds of memories are worth discussion. Some of the best conversations we have as a family are discussing our memories and telling stories about times gone by, and undoubtedly there will be disagreements over what happened or how it happened. But most importantly, there will be differences of opinion on the impact or the perceptions. This is where we come to realize that the truth hits us all according to our own journeys and according to what seeds God is planting in each of us. Our future activities, which He has planned, will be partly determined based on previous events. According to Shawn Achor, in his book *Before Happiness*, the brain receives eleven million pieces of information from our environment every second, but it can only process forty bits per second, which means it has to choose what tiny percentage of input to process and attend to and what huge chunk to dismiss or ignore.[1] The same realities can produce different memories and, therefore, different lives and filters. The plan of God is amazingly intricate, and He is masterful in orchestrating the music of our lives and those forty bits per second that do become our lives.

It's a good time here to think about the synoptic Gospels and how they are the story of Jesus's life, told by different people. If your memories start to have some discrepancies, remember that the most important part is the *theme*. The synoptic Gospels vary in detail because of the varied writers, but they are congruent in message and theme. Remember the eleven million bits of information but the fact that only forty is the brain's capacity? Matthew, Mark, Luke, and John all wrote, and each recorded what was important, from their own perspective.

As a pastor, one of my first talks, given to a group of students, was called "Here Comes the Boom." I looked at my own life and attempted, through God's provision, to piece together a life that from the back forward seemed to make little sense and would worry the owner of such a life. But in hindsight, I could see how God was using all the previous experiences in my life to come to the "boom"—the moment it all made sense. If you're like me, then you long for those boom moments from God. When we're lucky, we get one now and then. But the biggest boom comes the day we see Him face-to-face and everything falls into place. It's looking back and seeing those boom moments God gives us that grows our faith and strengthens our faith in Him.

THEMES

So, what else has my life been about? What themes and messages have come to pass as I look back with fifty-one-year-old eyes? (I had to change that because I was forty-nine when I started writing this.) There are a few that jump out at me that will come into play in my story and maybe connect you to this drama as well. John Eldredge will rightfully say that the greatest need in every person is to know "if I have what it takes."[2] As a child and then a young man, this need for affirmation and approval rang strong in my life. Second, I seemed to always be the hard worker. I was a good kid whom parents wanted their sons to hang out with, and I was affirmed in my compliance and goodness. With both my parents being educators, I knew the rules, I followed them, and I was the kid in the group project team who got upset at all the other teammates because they didn't do anything. Third, I was the black sheep of the group, class, family, and team; I always felt a bit off the mark. I was too athletic for the nerds, and I was too nerdy for the athletes. I didn't want to drink, but I wanted to be invited to the parties. I didn't have confidence in myself, but the teachers thought I was capable. I'm a heterosexual male, but I'm much more comfortable while small-talking with women. I didn't fit the molds that I thought existed. Finally, perhaps because of my black sheep feelings, I have always found myself caring for and about the underdog. I liked the nerds; I was the weakling, but I had a bit of a voice in my circles, and I wanted to use it. These are just some of the themes that play into my story. Men carry a multitude of themes, many being family-of-origin issues, especially father wounds. I'm sitting with a man now who introduced me to a whole new level of father issues. It's only by God's grace that he is as healthy as he is. In ministry especially, if you're a man, it's good to be fully aware of your father issues, and there is no more significant place for a father wound to be triggered than when working with a senior pastor or dominant elder—someone holding authority over you who can subconsciously take on that father role, and then let you down in his own brokenness or through daily life, which will reengage you with your unhealed wound.

I sat with a minister who was dealing with this very issue.

Having had his own father not fulfill many of his needs growing up, this father-figure boss, unbeknownst to him, had become the surrogate father. And once again, this "father" had let him down. Part of the battle is knowing the theme; the next stage is working through it. This minster has since left the ministry but has used the awareness to work on issues with his real father, and God has used his pain for good. Find a therapist and discuss your themes. Consider what path God has been paving in your life; look at how you handle life, what situations you always find yourself in; and identify problem behaviors or triggers. Often in ministry we live in the false assumption that ministry is pure and void of these triggers and problems. We live as if there is a spiritual bubble that keeps us protected from bad thoughts, ill manners, and wounds surfacing. But such is not the case. We are in the crosshairs of a spiritual battle, and this is very effective weaponry to be used by the enemy. Be aware.

I would even argue that in many churches, family-of-origin wounds are more likely to surface because the environment is very family-like. The corporate world has its issues, but it's often structured, processed, and laid out in such a way that certain things aren't discussed. You're OK not liking your coworkers or not respecting your boss. In the corporate world, you know the rules and there's a handbook. Talking about your feelings is taboo and awkward. But in some church settings, you're relating as if coworkers are brothers and sisters, and because it's church, it just seems like life should be good all the time. But we're still wounded. We're still broken. We're still human. Many family themes can surface in your church family. Remembering my childhood, my journey, and my themes has helped in my authentic look at who I am and what God has been doing in my life. This awareness gives meaning to situations, giving the clarity that we so often pray for God to reveal. It also helps us see others in new ways, sometimes to provide empathy and grace where we thought we would never be able to.

Time after time, I hear professionals in and out of ministry telling people not to look back, not to worry about the past. That concerns me, not because I want people to get stuck in the past, but because the past clarifies the future and helps us be more effective and healthier going forward. It's why we review game tape and why we assess our past performances. Why did I slice? Why do I always flinch when that happens? Why can't I take it over the finish line? We need to remember and understand what drives us, what stops us, and what has shaped our lives. Consider these questions in your own life, and start a journal on memories that come to mind as you read this story. Ask God to seek you, know you, and reveal in you what's going on in your world.

CHAPTER 2

RELATIONSHIPS

So, as the story develops, let's talk a little about human development. I want this chapter not only to inform you of your own life patterns but also to lay a foundation for the stories you hear in *Scream without Raising Your Voice* so that you will be able to connect the dots later. How we develop and how we grow is critical to the way we view life as adults and how we navigate the world. At one level, I think this developmental concept is simple and makes all the sense in the world, but I lose the context that a lot of people don't think in this way or haven't had any training in understanding the ways of human life. It's like when my MBA friends assume it's simple for everyone to calculate an ROI, or when my son explains server domains to me. And while we're at it, let's talk about bitcoin. I'm going to assume that talking about relationships is valuable to some of my readers—more valuable than their bitcoin investment.

From a psychotherapy perspective, the past is the present. What I mean by that is that what we experience, or perceive to experience, affects who we are and how we live. Our environment shapes us, and our mental composition sets us up to absorb or reject the environmental stimuli according to our predisposed nature. So, the question of nature versus nurture is simply answered by saying yes. Let me explain through a diagram I often use that I created based on a similar concept used by Bob Hamp, a fellow therapist and pastor. I've tweaked it and added my own language to it, but I give credit to him for the concept and original diagram. Let's start at the top. We will call it "Life Events."

In Life Events, we learn to read, write, eat, and walk, but we also learn how to deal with our emotions, learn if we have value, and assess if we are safe. And when I say we learn about these latter things, I mean that it's not usually an intentional process. It's commonplace that we focus on teaching academic and physical skills, but many times we fail to focus on the emotional and relational skills, which would really serve us well later in life if we were actually intentionally taught their nature in a healthy way. Were you intentionally taught how to manage your emotions when you were five? And by manage, I don't mean stuff your emotions, or to be quiet or else "I'll *give* you something to cry about." In addition to your emotions, what did you learn about yourself when you were ten? You may have even laughed when you read that question, but your ten year old experience is there, affecting you, nonetheless. Many times it is pain that grows us, teaches us, and imprints a belief onto us. What pain have you been through?

As we come to the next stop on our diagram, we find a spot called *cognitions*, or in simpler terms I'll say *beliefs*. Your learning from earlier in your life creates in you a set of beliefs that dictates how you see life, how you see yourself, and how you see others. John Eldredge uses the term *agreements*, whereas PTSD therapy uses the term *stuckpoints*. We could venture into a word such as *strongholds* or even the phrase *value system*. I like *agreements* myself, as this term doesn't necessarily connote a positive or negative reality (as, for example, *stuckpoints* does); agreements are just things that we tell ourselves are true about the world. Of course, this is where we realize that Satan is the one in charge of the negative agreements. We can see here how Satan uses our negative (or even positive) experiences in our circle of life, to tell us lies, and the feedback process of our diagram shows how his scandal is reinforced. Agreements are critically pivotal in dictating how we do life. Don't overlook this reality.

There's a powerful scene at the end of the version of *Wonder Woman* released in 2017 that I think does a great job of showing what this looks like in our lives. Diana ends up confronting Ares in the tower toward the end of the movie. In looking for an enemy she doesn't fully understand or recognize, she comes face-to-face with her unknown adversary. During the great reveal scene, Ares (the evil one) clarifies that he has spent years whispering into the ears of humans various ideas and inspirations for formulas and weapons, but he clarifies, saying that he never made them use them, adding that they "start these wars on their own." These beliefs are so critical to our behavior, we must be careful of what we believe and be aware of the source of our beliefs.

Heading to our next stop, we find the behavioral aspect of our diagram. We take our agreements, and we behave based on what we believe to be true and thereby create an *identity* based on that reality. Whatever our true identity is, we layer it with coping mechanisms and addictions to comfort us from the world that we experienced through life events and to protect us from what we think is to come. I had a guy tell me he was an introvert. It turns out that he wasn't an introvert at all, but he had taken on introversion, a coping mechanism, because he was taught that he was not worthy enough to give input. It's painful to give input and not be valued time and time again. It's painful enough to cause you to "put on" introversion. Maybe you are aggressive, or maybe you have acted aggressively because you've been taught that aggression was necessary to succeed. See the difference? Whatever persona we take on and wrap around our true selves, we take into the world.

Now that we think we know how the world works and we have created a new identity to take out into the world, we take our adaptive and maladaptive selves back into life events and we get feedback, the type of feedback that changes or affirms our *cognitions*. Then we change or reinforce our identity and go back out and get more feedback. This happens weekly, daily, and hourly in our lives, but most of us have never thought to think through it to see if we are OK with the cycle that we are living in. This concept is a pretty simple view of how life works. You can find a variety of similar diagrams with similar concepts in similar therapists' offices, but this is the one I use. Unfortunately, most of our foundational development happens between the ages of zero and twelve, during our most impressionable formative years, and we spend the rest of our lives living in it or crawling out of it. Unlearning is a critical skill to learn as an adult.

Here's the diagram with a few extra nuances added in:

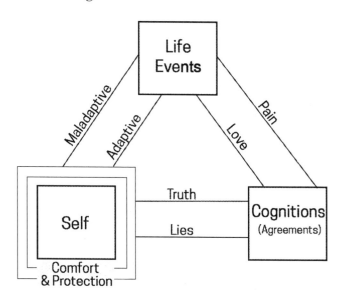

What does this look like in real life? John is a client who was unsupported by his parents when he was young because he never needed "supporting." He was a good kid who got good grades, and his parents never "had to" correct him or direct him. They didn't want to pressure him, so since he was doing well, they accepted that and, for the most part, left him alone. Their behavior made John feel he was not valuable and not worth encouraging. He said he could have done better, but no one seemed to care. John's older sister, ten years his senior, would often invite him along on her teenage outings and friend gatherings. He enjoyed the attention he got from older girls and even the older boys. What was imprinted in him as a learning young child was an agreement that he was not valuable to his parents and he wasn't worth investing in. Therefore, he needs to spend time investing in himself. Another agreement was that he needed to connect to older people, not same-age people, if he was to be accepted. Thirty years later, he is currently unable to connect with people his age; he lives with guilt from abandoning his own parents who, he felt, didn't value him; and he still has a hard time investing in himself. His identity is one of a businessman possessing a maturity beyond his years, yet he longs for same-age connection because, now in his forties, he doesn't have friends who understand his stage of life with young kids, only friends who understand retirement. He does not feel accepted for who he is and works for approval. It's a simple example of a very multifaceted and layered reality of life. Your story may show a similar pattern.

It's important to understand that your early life played a *huge* role in laying the foundation for your present life, and it's also important to understand that the process continues today. Each day, each experience, affects your beliefs and your identity, which is reinforcing, correcting, and modifying you. We have, in recent years, learned that our brains are neuroplastic and that they daily change into what we direct them to become. To illustrate this idea, you can insert any verse here, such as Philippians 4:8, which reminds us of the following:

Finally, brethren, whatsoever things are true, whatsoever things are honest, whatsoever things are just, whatsoever things are pure, whatsoever things are lovely, whatsoever things are of good report; if there be any virtue, and if there be any praise, think on these things.

It's amazing that God understands the way His creation works and has advised us accordingly. Unfortunately, many of us didn't get to choose what we focused on when we were kids. Some of us had to focus on survival or the abuse of others, and sometimes shame, fear, and insecurity were our focus, therefore becoming the nutrients that grew our brains.

Let's focus on a couple of those nutrients that are significant to childhood. Maybe you can do some soul-searching here and determine if you see yourself in the following descriptions:

ATTACHMENT THEORY

One of the more tangible things to look at is your attachment to your parents, especially your attachment to your mother. Coined as "attachment theory" by John Bowlby, a psychoanalyst in the mid-1900s, the theory examines how an infant is "attached" to his parents, as I mentioned, especially through the mother–child bond. There are four possible outcomes:

Secure attachment
This is the ideal type of attachment, where a child is securely attached and knows that safety exists at the hands of his or her parents. Anxious upon separation, these children are easily comforted upon return of their parent(s). As adults, they will be secure in their efforts and safe in who they are. They risk and fail in a healthy way and know that ultimately they are safe and

content in who they are. For someone in ministry, this could look like a person who is comfortable taking risks and failing as much as he or she succeeds, a person who doesn't get shaken when a teen's parents chew him out, a person who is able to take on a new role where success won't be likely for a while. Secure attachment lets you know that you are good regardless of the circumstance.

Anxious-Resistant Attachment

This category describes infants who had a greater level of distress when separated, but when reunited, they found both comfort and hostility or had a sense of wanting to punish the parent(s) for leaving. As adults, they crave emotional attention in their relationships and can often become clingy and undermine their own desires to be comforted and connected. Anxious-resistant ministry leaders can be codependent and people-pleasing, which is very dangerous in the church. Existing in a place where there are too many personalities and agendas to please can be overwhelming and exhausting and may produce manipulative relational strategies.

Avoidant Attachment

This describes infants who, when separated, showed low distress but also showed no interest in the parent(s) when reunited, or they actively sought to avoid the parent(s). As you can imagine, these adults are distant and self-focused. Their relationships struggle in connection and intimacy as the adults focus on their own needs and, in some cases, fear the connection that relationships bring. You can see for yourself, I assume, the challenge this person would have in authentic ministry roles.

Disorganized–Disoriented Attachment

This category, added to the list later, was designated to describe children who have no predictable pattern of attachment behaviors. It typically stems from parents who were not confident in their nurturing and who withdrew, then weakly acquiesced and tried to comfort. These children grow up with mixed signals and often take on a role reversal of the parent–child dynamic. They often will either find others to provide comfort in a way they never had experienced and disassociate from their own needs, or they may exhibit chaotic, dangerous behavior and withhold care from others.

All these attachment styles produce adults symptomatic of the nutrients they were fed. This is but a tiny glimpse into the world of attachments, but it will provide a huge glimpse into the world of your relationships and why you do what you do. I won't go into the details, as I don't necessarily want this to be a Psychology 101 book, but I encourage you to get better acquainted with attachment styles. I've had a number of clients borrow my books or search the internet and become enlightened.

Consider these styles as you consider your own behavior patterns relationally. What does the impact of your attachment style look like in your senior pastor or elder relationships? How about your co-pastors or staff? Understanding (not labeling) the way other people think about the world is powerful in helping you to understand why they do what they do. Often, it's not about you; it's about the other person's agreements, wounds, and experiences. These theories of attachment find real estate in your brain and affect the way you pastor, father, mother, parent, or be a friend and even how you respond to God and the goals He sets out before you. For more information on attachment theory, check out one or more of the number of good books on the market covering this topic—not only what attachment theory means, but also how to become securely attached if you feel you identify with one of the unsecure styles.

TEN RELATIONAL NEEDS

Another nutrient that feeds your personal world at an early age is how your relational needs were met. As I mentioned, we learned how to eat, drink, walk, and write, but what we don't realize is that we were also learning how we as human beings fit into the world: Do I have value? Does my voice matter? Am I worth investment or encouragement? And so on. Most of this is always going on in the background, yet when it's right in front of our faces, we're just ignorant to it. Unless your parent was a therapist trained in relational needs, odds are these things were "taught" by happenstance.

As humans, we are created to live in community and to grow in a healthy family unit. Ideally, those relationships meet needs within us that, when done well, provide mental nourishment and a healthy foundation from which to view life. Our agreements and our ways of dealing with life are formed at early ages and either haunt us or serve us well as we grow into adulthood. Most talk therapy centers on identifying these coping mechanisms and beginning an adjustment process on the maladaptive ones. It's in these relationships that we learn how to stay in an argument or run, how to speak up or assume we have no opinion that matters, and how to forgive or hold a grudge. As with wet concrete, people put their initials in your mind, and those can remain for life unless you undergo some significant reworking. I often share with my clients that a major part of healing is unlearning. We focus on learning new things, but it's truly in the unlearning of old things that breakthrough happens.

There are a number of sources on the relational needs theory, but I draw from a 1994 publication from Intimacy Press on the top ten needs.[3] I just read a book where the author describes using seven relational needs with his clients. I don't think there's a right answer, but mine seems a little more thorough than his. Just saying. ☺ Actually, we tend to do as we are taught, and this is the model I and my colleagues use at our practice. My method is to provide a printout with a minor description of each term and then ask the client to rank each parent, in each category, from 0 to 10 on a Likert scale. Feel free to do the same in your head or in your copy of this book. And remember, we are looking at those formative years from zero to twelve.

Comfort   Mother _____ Father _____

Was comfort provided when you were hurt, scared, or disappointed? Did someone show concern for you and take your emotions seriously? When you lost the spelling bee or your girlfriend broke it off with you, were you told to "get over it," or rather did someone say, "I'm sorry. That's got to be painful for you," and sit with you?

I want to pause here and say that a high number is not always better than a low number; both can have a good or bad result, but ideally you want the number to be higher. Highly comforted people can, in some cases, grow up and need that same level of comfort from Mom or Dad, who isn't there anymore, and they are unable to find it in themselves or in the mean world. They can become needy and sensitive. It can be difficult for them to deal with the hardships of life. Low-comforted people may find it hard to seek solace in community or a spouse and might not share emotions because they received no reward when young. And often, low-comforted people have no sympathy for the highly comforted people. Conflict ensues.

Acceptance   Mother _____ Father _____

When we are children, we need to know that we are accepted in spite of our oddities or strange desires. Whether it's a physical defect or mental or academic struggle, our parents can look beyond our faults, differences, and irritating characteristics to see our worth. Someone put it, "It's an unconditional acceptance of an imperfect person." We are all imperfect people. Many parents, however, unknowingly communicate, *If you were different, I would love you.*

Affection   Mother _____ Father _____

This one is often tough for men because they were raised to be tough. They raise their kids to be tough, and so on and so on—the cycle continues. But men desire to know that they are loved. We need this type of assurance from our moms and our dads. It signifies that we are worthy of being loved—that we are lovable. Knowing that we are lovable and worth loving pays big dividends when we are looking for relationships of our own. A parent verbalizing "I care for you," "I'm here for you," and "I love you" is critical here.

Appreciation   Mother _____ Father _____

In this one, we focus on what is *done*. Many of us remember when growing up doing our chores with this being expected, not appreciated. Being appreciated for doing your homework, for obeying the first time, and for waiting patiently all signify that you are appreciated for your efforts. Appreciative parents never take a child's efforts for granted, noticing the big and small things that are done, focusing on the positive efforts, not the negative flaws. If you lived in a world where you were not appreciated just for doing "what you were supposed to do," you can feel unappreciated and taken for granted. This isn't about appreciating the above and beyond, but about being on the receiving end of regular gratitude.

Approval   Mother _____ Father _____

Whereas appreciation is focused on the doing, approval is focused on the *being*. By recognizing the uniqueness of a person and being OK with who he or she is being, that person learns that he or she has value outside his or her efforts. Approval differs from acceptance in that approval is being OK with who you *choose* to be. Acceptance is being OK with who you *are* at the core of your existence and character formation. To the naked eye, this can look a little odd as we see parents being OK with strange hair or body piercings, or being accepting of dress style and career choices.

These parents are meeting one of the desires of their child's heart, which is to know that he or she is unconditionally approved of—just as our heavenly Father loves us.

Let me pause here and clarify three of these in simpler terms, in case too many words made it too confusing.

Acceptance
You are OK the way God made you, even if you are artsy, silly, serious, creative, analytical, "not like your brother," etc.

Approval
"I love you regardless of your choices." This is the opposite of being shamed or purposefully embarrassed. Green hair is not my idea of a good choice, but if you are my child and you have green hair, I approve of you even if you choose to do that.

Appreciation
"I appreciate what you do." "Thank you for taking the trash out." "Thank you for helping your sister."

Attention   Mother _____ Father _____
Did your parents express an interest in being with you? Did they listen to your opinions and engage in conversation with you? Attention is all about being together, doing things together. It's about interest without criticism and making time for the other person. Whether you feel that your opinion matters or if you are invisible depends on the attention you receive or do not receive. We all need attention. We have a desire to be seen. We have a desire to be known.

Respect   Mother _____ Father _____
Honor is a good partner word for *respect*. Did you feel honored growing up by getting the dignity you deserved? This looks like not being put down in front of others. Sarcasm can often be

a violation of a person who needs respect; hurtful and harsh criticism does the same. Being respected is also about having your opinion taken seriously and being valued at age-appropriate levels.

Encouragement   Mother _____ Father _____
The word itself helps us see that there is a need for others to put courage into us. When you doubted or had fears, did anyone make the effort to give you the strength to overcome the obstacle ahead or to win the battle against what you were fearing? Encouragement shows that you are valued and teaches you that you can rely on others and that relationships are good.

Support   Mother _____ Father _____
Support ties back to our attachment theory discussion about knowing that you have a safe base and a strong foundation to rely on. When needed, there is a rescue and help is available. It's with this support that you find your strength to take risks and fail in a healthy way. Sometimes tasks are shared here to let you know that sharing burdens is important.

Security   Mother _____ Father _____
This is the foundational need, knowing that it's OK to express yourself, to disagree, and to share your opinions without rejection or criticism. Security gives you a voice and confirms that it's OK to be you and to share you, the way God made you, with others. If you are secure, then you won't be cast out, you won't have to do without, and you won't be rejected and exiled. Without security, you have very little.

All of these are important, but security is what I find to be the most important of them all. It's foundational to all the other needs, and if it's not met, the brain can do little to focus on the others. I have a friend who is the postadoption director at an institution that facilitates the adoption of babies to families.

His main role is to educate, coach, and console parents who are sometimes parents for the first time, and many who are parents of an adopted child for the first time. As he educates, he spends a healthy amount of time helping parents understand that many of these kids did not come from a secure environment. As he lays out the brain structure and helps them understand that when the amygdala is constantly telling the hippocampus to assume the worst and prepare for fight, flight, or freeze, there is no room for anything else. The body shuts down the ability to receive comfort, affirmation, and all the other needs because the children are focused on survival. This model mirrors Maslow's hierarchy of needs, which postulates that we cannot process relationship and intimacy unless our physiological needs (air, water, food) and our safety needs (personal security, health, and well-being) are met. It's one of the reasons school counselors are focused on the well-being of the underprivileged children and why free lunches are offered. You can't learn a thing or relate to others if you are worried about where your next meal will come from.

It's also important to realize that I could have ended the description of every need by writing "just like our heavenly Father does for us." He will meet these needs, but when we are age four, he has given us parents to teach us how to receive those things from Him later and also how to give them to others. Unfortunately, as broken humans in a world that is falling fast, we often fail to fulfill this role we have been given.

MY TOP THREE

It is said that even though we all have all ten needs, there are two or three that will rise to the top for each of us, sort of like finding one's personal love language. There will be needs that seem to have an extra pull for you, as if your body has a deficiency of iron or something else. You will crave these needs more than the others. For me, my top three are approval, encouragement, and support. As I said earlier, I've always found myself a little different from others. I imagine most everyone says that. I've never met anyone who says, "I'm just like all the other people, and I feel great." On one level, we want to be the same; on another level, we want to be whomever God made us to be. I don't think that second level materializes until later in life.

Although I have never struggled with same-sex attraction, I always could relate to women better than to men for sure. I wasn't a hunter, or a motorcycle-riding, alcohol-drinking, cigarette-smoking man's man. I understand that there are millions of us out there, but day in and day out I just felt that I was an anomaly. These are my school years I'm referring to. I was athletic and relatively attractive, so I was cool enough to have an audience with young men of that type, but I was also smart enough and benign enough that I had an audience with the nerds. I was never fully comfortable in either camp, so I bounced between the two and felt lost in the middle. In elementary school, I was a little more on the nerd side with some athleticism, and in high school I was a little more of an athlete with a nerdy side. I was dancing on either side of the center point of confusion, trying to be OK with who I was. Approval was big.

Many times, I find clients with purpose or motivation based on a theme in life. Whether it's their own trauma mastery or a coping mechanism, I see this play out time and time again—the abused mother who feels she needs to worry about her staff, or the devalued young woman who continually hooks up with less-than-stellar men. These are themes that tell us about ourselves and our story.

I assume my theme came from my connection with the nerds and even perhaps my own experiences being bullied in school. I didn't like the way the nerds were treated, and I didn't like the way I was treated. I remember a time when a grade school neighbor harassed me at the bike rack at school. He was the typical short insecure bully, but he sent me home crying to my mother and wondering why I wasn't able to handle myself in that situation. I did have my growth spurt in seventh grade, and even though I never really developed much upper-body strength, I was tall early. If you include my five inches of eighties hairdo, I was huge. As mentioned earlier, I often found myself advocating for the underdog. Perhaps it was the love of Christ in me that was growing a seed of compassion as well. Something in me was growing, but like most of our motivations, we often don't see them until later in life. As I look back, I specifically remember sitting outside the room at a house party in high school, worrying about the young woman inside who was with a young man whom I knew (felt) was not interested in her but only in what she might be willing to offer him that evening. People being mistreated was not appropriate, but given my insecurities, I did nothing really but wait and worry. I was frustrated with the jocks who came to church each Sunday morning after a Saturday night of debauchery. They were arrogant and self-centered, in my mind, and I was not mature enough to know they were dealing with their own issues. But the theme was well under way. Perhaps somewhere in there I was jealous of muscles, or accolades, or girlfriends, but regardless, I was drawing my allegiance against the grain and establishing my own worldview that would later affect my relationships.

SELF-ASSESSMENT

You may have assessed your own needs as you read through this, but if you haven't done so, I would challenge you to go back and do it. When you were growing up, how was your worldview set? What were your agreements? Were your needs met adequately or too adequately? Perhaps you didn't have a father at all, or perhaps yours was a house of chaos and fear. And if your needs weren't met, how did you compensate? Did you get them met in maladaptive ways? Did you try to convince yourself you didn't require a particular need be met? Or maybe you told yourself you didn't deserve it anyway. Sit in the answers to these questions for a little bit and see where God leads your memories. Invite Him into the thought process and see what surfaces. I pray that you have awareness, but it may be that you need outside perspective from a professional.

I also want you to consider identifying themes. When I say this, I don't mean something such as "I always wanted to be a dentist when I grew up." Rather, focus on emotional things like relational struggles. Thoughts aren't easily dispelled. To help you get started, I'll mention a few areas that come to mind, especially for men: "I'm never good enough"; "I always find myself as the party initiator"; "No one calls me"; "I'm always trying to move toward the movers and shakers"; and "I always gravitate to the oppressed." Sit in this for a few days or weeks. Ask God to reveal your themes, and try to identify the thread that runs through your life. Often, the themes aren't positive. More often, they seem positive at first, but once you look at them honestly, you find they aren't.

Many times, our themes can come from trauma that has never been processed, wounds that have never healed. Lean into those and see what God reveals. We spend our time avoiding things so that we can stay productive and not let such stuff bog us down. But I think that in doing so, we never deal with what needs to be dealt with. It keeps festering, we keep "not letting it affect us," and the theme continues. For many of us, there is a significant theme in our life, generated from the past, in alignment with an agreement, that we refuse to acknowledge. It is one that is causing issues, creating friction, and keeping us from having healthy relationships and being the true self God has designed us to be.

Speaking of themes, my son will disagree with this analogy, so do your best with it. One of my family's favorite places to go is to Lake City, Colorado, to a little inn at the shore of

Lake San Cristobal in the San Cristobal mountain range. It's a terrifying mountain ride (for me—remember, not a man's man) over Cinnamon Pass to Silverton, and a much safer but longer ride along the Silver Thread Byway. The Silver Thread Byway takes you through beautiful valleys and between mountains. It's just one of those locations where you just feel that you're in the right place. On a motorcycle, it's a front-peg cruise; in your car, it's a refreshing break from burning brakes and trying to avoid dangerous drop-offs. But some people continue to go over the pass and up the side of the mountain—the six-foot-wide path accommodating an eight-foot-wide truck, for example—where they confront people who have to back up, creating friction and scaring the drivers' wives, because something in these people drives them to pursue that theme in life. It doesn't make any good sense from the outside, but people continue to do it. Just like our aggression, jealousy, and avoidance, conflicts drive us from some place deep inside, when there's a better way to live.

I prefer the Silver Thread Byway through your life, which God has been paving for years, waiting for you to cruise on with Him. It doesn't mean it's not at high elevations and that there won't be a falling rock now and again, but it does mean that He is ready for you with His plantings and His paving. It's from that area of security, knowing who you are in Him, that your true identity gives you the strength to get through an avalanche, navigate falling rocks, and get on with life, knowing that you have a secure attachment in Him, your Father. Step away from that theme of anger, insecurity, or whatever, and establish that secure attachment in Him. Relationships are driven by relationships, past and present.

"Why a chapter on relationship?" you ask. "That's a lot of psychobabble!" As I sit with laypeople, with pastors, and with myself, I come to realize that many of our traumas arise through relational struggle and conflict between people. Emotions, feelings, and matters of the heart come into play, so to effectively understand your trauma and get past it, to see what God is doing and has done in your life, you must understand why we people do what we do and what we can do about it. As I share with some of my guys, we need to understand what forces are at play around and within us and what the rules of the game are that we are expected to be effective at playing. You cannot pastor, father, mother, parent or be a friend as well as you would like if you don't understand what forces are at play in your world. Satan is fully aware of these forces, and he uses that knowledge like a skilled assassin.

To heal from trauma requires a journey inward. Understanding *whose* you are and *who* you are is critical.

CHAPTER 3

REVEALING

I enjoyed my high school girlfriend for several wholesome reasons. She was a good person, probably better—no, definitely better—than I was as a human being. But one of the things that solidified in my mind, something I have told of over and over again, is the reality of pastoral life. Many of us, maybe I can say most of us, tend to put pastors on this pedestal of authority, respect, and perfection. The reality is that many people worship their pastors more than they worship God. My girlfriend was a PK (preacher's kid) before I even knew what a PK was. I was privy to an insider's view of church life and the realness of doing life as a pastor family. As I said, it was a very formative and foundational time in my life. The reality is, her dad wasn't worthy of worship. He was (is) a great human being, and her mom was (is) a great woman as well. Their family had very normal struggles and disagreements, and a diverse group of children, but God was still part of it. If you don't relate, then I like to say that it's kind of like being a twelve-year-old and seeing your teacher at the store buying toilet paper. You come to realize that pastors (and teachers) are real people with their own challenges going on. Maybe this was a seed for me; maybe this was a theme emerging.

So, when do you know you're called into ministry? For some

it happens young and they plan their lives around it. For some it surfaces later, as was the case for me. In the Protestant Church, there are many opportunities to serve in the ministry without a formal theology degree. Some readers may have an issue with that; this issue is not for discussion here. But I do think that my not having a theology degree was one more affirmation of my black sheep identity. But in reality, who doesn't feel like a black sheep sometimes?

CONSTRUCTING A FUTURE

I had spent twelve years working my way up the corporate ladder, and as I continued to grow in my faith, grow in my profession, and grow in my family, I had a gut feeling that this was not the silver thread of a path that God wanted me on. As I continued up the ladder, I had feelings that I was growing out of who I was and growing into some shadow of myself, into an area of discontent and inadequacy. Going back to my formulation of my life as a young man, I saw that my path was to be very obedient to the expectations of other people. I was a good person, a hard worker, obedient, and a rule follower. But deep down in the core of my being, I was creative, emotional, spiritual, and relational, and I felt that the world was getting less and less receptive to someone with those core desires as time went on. I had less time for the hobbies that once had allowed me to express these things. I had fewer opportunities to make a positive impact on people through those hobbies. My ability to do them, because of my stresses and perceived expectations, had lessened. It seemed as if the core of who I was, was being threatened by the reality of who I was trying to be. God was on the move.

With the time I did have, I was serving in my local church in this season. God was moving there as well. I was assisting the team responsible for the weekend service elements—tech and creative arts—and my education was in facilities and real estate. For the company where I worked, I had successfully accomplished everything from managing building usage, vendors, leases, and land acquisitions to negotiating contracts, managing construction, and overseeing security. In the early stages of this local church, it was growing because the area around us was being developed. It was obvious that we needed a new building, and we needed one fast. Growth was happening all around.

As many churches do, we chose to hire from within. In October 2006, I was asked if I would be willing to come on, full time, as a pastor to manage all that I was already helping with and to oversee the new building. It was time for me to pray.

SIGNS FROM GOD

Probably one of the most asked, most pondered questions I receive from men, or really people in general, is "How do I know if I heard from God? How do I know if it was Him, or me, or Satan, or Uncle Gary who put that thought in my head?" Great question; keep asking it. As mentioned earlier, I'm not a theologian, so I can only speak from experience and others' wisdom, but I do know that the more you ask that question and the more you lean into God and let Him reveal Himself to you, the easier it is to discern His voice. Consider your own father.

Many of us have a phrase or some colloquialism that we grew up with. In our house, my dad always said, "It's always something." And he didn't say this with a happy smile of expectancy, it was sort of an Eeyore "I can't catch a break" delivery. His delivery conveyed the sense that there was always going to be something wrong in life. I had a young man tell me his dad always says, "You're just along for the ride," which conveyed to him that you get what you get, and you don't have the right to speak into this world. Of course, all these experiences play into our needs and set up themes in our lives, but they are also revealing of the character of our fathers. For those of us who know our fathers, there is an understanding, an intimacy, that lets us know what they like, what they think, and what they want. For those of us who don't know our fathers, we can only guess or assume what they want and what their desires are.

How well do you know your heavenly Father? Do you know what makes His heart beat? what His desires are? If someone were to pull up beside you in a car and say, "Your dad wants you to get in and come with me," would you believe the person? Or would you know that your dad would never do that without calling you first or letting you know the plan? The best way to get a good understanding of what God wants from you is to get a good understanding of God—to talk to Him frequently, to ask questions, to listen, to trust. Relationship and intimacy come from vulnerability and humility. But what if your dad really does want you to get into the car? Sometimes, God does ask people to do some seemingly odd things.

John Eldredge, in *Walking with God*, plays it out like this: When you think you hear something that is confusing, ask.[4] We forget that we are in a relational relationship with a conversational father. Throw it to Him. "Lord, did I hear this right? I think what You said was that I should get into the car." It reminds me of our reflective counseling technique: "What I hear you saying is this. Is that right?"

The Bible is full of people responding immediately, and we ourselves get wrapped up in the fear of thinking we have little faith or that we doubt too much, but it's OK to have a clarifying conversation with God. The Bible also has stories of people who wrestle with God. There are people who discuss and question and listen and reply. I believe there's a lot more noise in the world now, and while it's OK to seek clarification, it's best not to use lack of clarity as a hindrance to obedience.

When you get to know your Father, you'll know his favorite sayings, such as the following:

> Jesus said unto him, Thou shalt love the Lord thy God with all thy heart, and with all thy soul, and with all thy mind. This is the first and great commandment. And the second is like unto it, Thou shalt love thy neighbor as thyself. (Matthew 22:37–39)

There's a good chance that what you hear in opposition to that may be from your uncle Gary.

MANY OPTIONS

I throw this in just because it came to mind as I was typing. Another prominent issue I see in a believer's navigation of life is this overarching and oppressive thought that there is one magical path that God has laid out for us and that the blessings of a wonderful life come when we hear correctly and choose the correct door to open. Please don't promote this idea. Our directive from God is to love Him, worship Him, love others, and introduce others to His love. Period. The Bible is full of how to do these things. Whether we do this as a teacher, or a blogger, or a doctor, or an artist, or whatever is up to our choosing according to our bent and desires. If you're trying to decide if God wants you in California or Seattle as if one's wrong and the other is right, stop thinking that way. Spend some time throwing out the options to God and seek His input. But if He chooses to remain silent, don't fret. Just know that He gives you freedom, and His desire is that you trust Him no matter what, especially on the unclear path.

If you are trying to decide which of two things you prefer, ask yourself which one you want to go do, and then go do that one if you truly have received no word from God as to which is right. But when you move toward what you desire, act in such a way that He is your desire. That's the directive we have been given: seek first the kingdom.

SOMETHING TO SIT ON

I do believe that God speaks today. My favorite way of hearing His Word is through the coincidence of repetition. I'm definitely one of those people who needs to hear things more than once to remember them. Unlike my son, whose photographic memory and intelligence helps him excel, I am a "repeat, study, repeat, talk about it" kind of guy, which is what I must do to get my brain to assign information some value making it worthy of memorizing. And I believe that God orchestrates the will of His kingdom, so I'm deeply moved and motivated when I perceive what could be considered almost eerie recurrences of themes. I have learned to be especially alert to and especially aware of things that keep popping up in my life. A single thought can be a scary and unsafe thing to put your efforts behind, but when God orchestrates a three-legged stool of perspective or one with even more legs, it's worth sitting on it for a while. I often wonder how people get a three-legged perspective when they have only one leg of input. If your sole source of input is a weekend service, then it's hard to get "coincidences" to occur. You're limiting God's ability to wow you when you limit your exposure to Him. I think that's one of the greatest values to being connected to a community group, and a same-gender accountability group, and also to your personal journey of being in the Word and reading other literature; the occurrence of divine coincidences. Because I'm such a routine person, I try to oppose the routine and keep things fluid by sometimes reading books and articles and sometimes listening to podcasts, but always in community. When a random podcast, an unconnected conversation in my men's group, and a chapter of an unrelated book all communicate the same thought, it's definitely something to take to God.

BUTTON YOUR PANTS

Sometimes it's our own filter that keeps us from understanding what God is telling us. Here's a wonderful example of misinterpretation: My wife is a special education teacher. Amid all the blessings that come from this job, there are struggles as well, and they seem to be growing as this population grows, the bureaucracy deepens, and the red tape thickens. To add a little lightness to their days at work, my wife and her fellow special education teacher friend often enjoy telling each other stories about what happened with students they know and love in the course of their busy and interesting workdays. So, we'll say this story is about Garrett.

As a five-year-old kid with autism spectrum disorder, Garrett was conversational and loving but not fully cognizant of life, which made him both challenging and refreshing. It'd been a long day at school, and the bus was arriving to pick up the kids and take them back into their challenging worlds where things didn't always make sense, but they did their best. As the bus was seen approaching, the teacher told the kids to grab their backpacks and come line up. As Garrett approached, the teacher looked at him and said, "Garrett, button your pants." He nodded compliantly and did nothing. Once more, the teacher spoke up and said firmly, "Garrett, button your pants." Again, a compliant nod and no action on Garrett's part. Frustrated, the teacher approached him and bent down to his level, as all good teachers do, and said, firmly and slowly, "Garrett ... button ... your ... pants," because she knew he could do it and she knew he understood her. Exasperated, Garrett, this five-year-old Aspie, effectively communicated back to the teacher, in no uncertain terms, that his butt *was* in his pants and he had no idea what she wanted to him to do. He couldn't get it more in his pants. And such is life.

Like you, I sometimes mishear what God says. Sometimes it doesn't make sense in my filters, from my perspective, but that's why I seek repetition. It's also why we measure it against scripture and ask the Holy Spirit to guide us in our interpretation of thoughts and emotions. We compare it to our Father's desires, which we know to be true.

MY SIGNS

Now back to my prayerful consideration of a ministry position in the fall of 2006, it was my first significant "seek an answer from God" time in my life. I was a thirty-seven-year-old, establishing for myself a pretty significant place in the corporate world with advancement on the horizon, and I was asked to put it all aside to "study the Word of God for a living." Was the Old Testament furniture prophecy about to come true? There are three specific times I feel I heard from God as I sought answers.

Confession: I fear sharing my stories with you because more than a decade has passed and the intangible pieces have faded a bit. I have facts, but little feelings remain, and my gifts as a writer likely won't do justice to the moment, so I trudge ahead with insecurity and trepidation.

LEG ONE

As corporate roles often require, I was headed to a staff development training to be a better leader, a better employee, and a better person and, honestly, just to check the box that said I had completed it. Exercise after exercise was conducted while we sat there, and then a final exercise came to pass where we were asked to separate into groups based on our answers to a question. The question was a hypothetical scenario: "You have made evening commitments to a nonprofit organization for the next four weeks, of which your boss is aware. Work picks up, and your team needs you to work late and maybe even travel. Do you stay true to your commitment at the nonprofit, or would you apologize and back out of your commitment so that you can meet the demands of your job?"

After everyone had read it and completed their answers, the trainer asked us to divide up in the room and go stand in our respective groups. I don't remember how many people were in the training session, but I do remember how many people stood in my group with me. Zero. Zero people said they would stay true to their commitment to a nonprofit at the risk of losing their jobs. I'm not sure if that was a true assessment or if it was just what everyone pretended in order to look good for the company, but I do know that I did not belong in that environment. I was different. I was set apart. I had one good leg under me, but it wasn't enough.

LEG TWO

I especially like it when God uses a new experience that is outside of my routine to communicate with me. It felt as if there was a shift in the universe to make this clear for me. Details fail me as to location, but suffice it to say that I found myself reading an article in a magazine I had never read. It was the August 2006 edition of *Texas Monthly*, which I found in a waiting room or perhaps my parents' house—not sure, really. It was an obscure article about Highland Park Methodist Church—basically a one-page article with a one-column close on the following spread. It was a story of a story really, a story the pastor had shared about a nineteen-year-old man by the name of Kyle Hancock, who had signed a lucrative pitching deal with the Colorado Rockies, but then a short time later went home, forwent the money, and announced that he didn't want to be a baseball player. He enrolled in college and got involved in community service projects. The story went on to explain that he felt he was being honest about who he was and that he was no longer going to live out the expectations of his mother, grandfather, and coaches, who were greatly disappointed in his decision. Kyle's thought, and soon mine, was that he could find and shape the future that suited his aspirations better than he could while sitting in the bullpen of life. I heard God talking.

So, remember that I had been asked to leave my corporate job and go into full-time ministry. I could have been at first prompting and "yes, sir" obedient, or—as ultimately I chose to do—I could spend a season in prayer and throw the idea out to God, seeking His feedback. Maybe I'm weak in my faith, or perhaps my risk-averse personality takes me to this path, but I feel that significant life-changing events need prayer and contemplation. I try to be first-time responsive when I hear "Pay for that woman's dinner" or "Turn around and see if those people need help." Obedience is important, but wise counsel and prayer is also recommended to make sure that we are not emotionally responsive or focused on our own selfish motives. It is between you and God how you handle this sort of thing, but this is my story. I needed a third leg before I was going to move.

LEG THREE

Unsolicited, I was invited to a luncheon by one of our vendors. I like to call it a "fancy luncheon" because I wasn't a fancy person. I didn't know what it was or what it was about, but I had been asked because the fancy people in my organization weren't available, and it was free, and there might be special people there. So, I went. At the time, I wasn't looking for a third leg to my stool of faith. I just went during this season of contemplation and prayer.

It turns out the fancy luncheon people were hosting two authors who had cowritten a book entitled *Succeed on Your Own Terms*. We all left with a copy; I still have mine today. Herb Greenberg and Patrick Sweeney spent an hour telling stories from their book about people who had left their "normal" jobs and went on to make great impacts on the world doing what they loved and what they felt they had been designed to do. They had left the hamster wheel and had found their Silver Thread Byway. Are you kidding me?

I left that function and was hardly able to talk to my wife on my BlackBerry through the tears coming down my face. I was crying because I knew that God had spoken to me through that luncheon. It wasn't just what was said; it was that it hit me in emotional ways that could not be explained. I sobbed and talked and sobbed and talked and knew what needed to be done. It was the hardest thing I have ever done, yet it was the easiest decision, thanks to the stool God had given me to sit on. I was going to become a pastor.

As we close the "Past" section of *Scream without Raising Your Voice*, I challenge you to think through your past and identify the various things mentioned so far. Begin, if you haven't already done so, thinking about your motivations and emotions as you interact with people. Think about the people who irritate you, those who are hard to be around. Do you know why you find them troublesome? Really?

Before we continue, I want you to know that *Scream without Raising Your Voice* is heavy on the relational trauma discussion as that's the population I work with now and is a place where my story had a lot of relevance. You may be struggling with low funding, understaffing, or things that don't exactly fit this discussion. If so, I would still encourage you to continue reading this work as a primer on human behavior and to gain insight into what you would do if such a thing ever were to happen to you. My bet is you will find something familiar. Find a nugget of info you can use now and some wisdom to hold onto for the future.

PART II

PRESENT

CHAPTER 4

REVEREND

The Franciscan monk Richard Rohr, in his audiobook *True Self, False Self*, which is actually a collection of lectures, shares that we are all born with the priesthood of God in us.[1] We are made in His image, and we are made to worship Him. Unfortunately, at a young age, undereducated about spirituality, we feel special but cannot quite make sense of this. But that sense of specialness is what drives us to want to be great ballplayers, singers, activists, or lawyers—something to reconcile and make sense of this specialness we feel. I don't know that this is a universally true statement, but I know for me it resonated because I did feel that I was set apart, that I was special in ways that I and others couldn't understand. Perhaps it was this very feeing I was dealing with. It was what fueled my desire to serve in the ministry and answer the calling. But without formal training in the seminary, it would be a challenge.

UNDERSTANDING THE PASTOR

If you talk to those in the ministry, they will say that you can't understand what it's like being a pastor until you are one. You will likely nod your head and not believe a word of it. Being a pastor is a job; you have tasks, expectations, and coworkers. What's the big deal? My guess is that many who sign up have no idea of the unwritten job description that comes with the role at any level of ministry. Because the assertion that a person cannot know what it's like being a pastor until becoming one is actually a very true statement, and it's very hard to put into words how being a pastor is uniquely different.

When we launched Perissos, our ministry for those in ministry, I myself was having a hard time effectively communicating the role of a pastor, my own job, and why being a pastor so often becomes a stumbling block. There are many facets to the story, from too many diverse roles to understand and fill to too many and too unrealistic expectations. And we mustn't forget the very true reality that we pastors are significant targets for Satan's battle plan. If you are doing life without this reality of spiritual warfare squarely in your mind, which many Western churches are seemingly living in denial of, then you are significantly unprepared for your road ahead.

The place where I found the most helpful and clearly communicated concerns I wanted to help with, and be helped with myself, was in a *Christianity Today* article entitled "Everyone's Pastor, No One's Friend."[2] This enlightening article, written by Arthur P. Boers, sheds powerful light on the uniqueness of ministry and what I believe is one of the greatest threats to our pastors—loneliness. Giving him full credit, I've replicated his bullet list here for our discussion, but the content of his points has been generalized from his first-person account, and I've added my own clarifications. Why does a pastor, surrounded by hundreds or even thousands of people, live a life of loneliness?

If you're not a pastor, but rather an elder or congregation member, I hope this section enlightens you on what your pastor goes through and gives you the idea that maybe there is room for grace and understanding that has yet been given to him or her. Maybe as an elder you could consider leaving *Scream without*

Raising Your Voice, with a bookmark on this page, on the seats of your congregation members or in their mailboxes to build a healthier understanding of what it's like to take this role.

Working Alone

Pastors often do most of their work on a self-directed schedule and according to the flexibilities of their schedule. Granted, interruptions do occur, but pastors mostly set their own meetings, create their own schedules, and make countless judgment calls on what are the right or next things to do. Such "freedom" and self-guidance lends itself to loneliness, sort of like a child who is given free rein and respect when what he or she needs and craves is some direction, support, and guidance. I have clients who speak of their parents who never punished them and just trusted them to do what was right. These people never got into trouble at home when they were children, so they never got direction—a case of good kids receiving bad parenting. When we extend freedom along the lines of "I trust you to do the right things" and we close our doors and get to work, certain other people may feel this as unloving and uncaring. I admit that I struggle with this in many of my roles. I may need to touch base with leadership to make sure I have been seen and heard. As a pastor, when you are competent to do what you have been hired to do, you are often left to yourself to complete the task. Many people love this, but maybe you do not (remember our relational needs and attachment theory). Understanding your abandonment, trust, and attachment issues would be powerful here. Considering the needs of others, if you haven't already, is, in my mind, critical as well.

Lack of Reciprocation

A pastor is often sought out for wisdom, guidance, and direction, but there is no process for him to receive the same. Unless otherwise coordinated, there is no mentor, confidant, or confessor whose expertise a pastor can draw upon. Depending upon your role, you are often seen as the final authority, and depending upon your organizational structure, you may not have an elder team, pastoral mentor, coach, or counselor to assist you. You need to actively work against this and make sure you are positioned next to and under others.

Our Frailties
People often acknowledge that pastors are "only human," but they also don't really want to know about their shortcomings or failures. They somehow assume (or want to believe) that pastors have harnessed all the powers of God and overcome the human issues. I'm thankful to see more pastors being vulnerable onstage with their own insecurities, depression, and shortcomings because I think it helps people overcome their own shame. It lowers the bar to a realistic level of humility. More importantly, it focuses people on God as their Redeemer, not their pastor as their redeemer. But unless you've built a culture to receive this knowledge, the risk of loss of your followers or supporters, or whatever you think you have, will play loudly in your mind to keep you quiet. And what if this role is fulfilling within you a relational need of approval? Then you just squelched your willingness to share.

Paul, however, shares this:

> And lest I should be exalted above measure through the abundance of the revelations, there was given to me a thorn in the flesh, the messenger of Satan to buffet me, lest I should be exalted above measure. For this thing I besought the Lord thrice, that it might depart from me. And he said unto me, My grace is sufficient for thee: for my strength is made perfect in weakness. Most gladly therefore will I rather glory in my infirmities, that the power of Christ may rest upon me. (2 Corinthians 12:7–9)

Paul is not pretending as if he doesn't struggle with depression, or doesn't struggle with an urge to use pornography, or doesn't struggle with pride; rather, he is admitting that whatever it is, he has prayed against it and it has not been taken from him so that God can be seen as sufficient. As a sidenote, this is a good time to point out that "being spiritual enough" or "having stronger faith" isn't necessarily what gets your prayers answered.

Playing the Role of Pastor
Boers states that when asked "How are you really doing?" from someone who cares, he is easily caught off guard and isn't sure how to respond based on the issues previously discussed. In my own world, I've seen pastors afraid to be authentic because of the culture of the church or the expectations of their leadership. There is a created incongruence within a person that leads to identity crisis and a subconscious need to stay away from people to avoid this ethical confrontation. Avoiding people is not where a pastor needs to be; rather, he needs to be in a supportive relationship with loving individuals.

Isolation from Extended Family
Depending on denomination and organizational structure, some pastors, not given a choice of where they pastor, end up in a place away from family and whatever friends and roots they had. This family is often the only group of people whom they can really be genuine with, without fear of consequence. Church staff can become like family, but I'll discuss issues with that later. Isolation is very real. My organization does the psychological church staff assessment for church plant organizations. It is critical that this support system and any need thereof be assessed. Sending a pastor and his spouse to a new state or town without at least assessing this need in him and what his options are is foolish. Many churches don't consider it or support it and aren't even aware of it. Isolation easily creates loneliness.

Social Isolation

To further this point on isolation, I created a new bullet point out of Boers's Isolation from Extended Family bullet point. A pastor's social isolation warrants its own description, in my opinion. Boers notes that church work takes up most of his socializing energy but doesn't fulfill his companionship needs. In fact, pastoring can actually hinder socializing. I have little time to meet "outsiders." In other words, we pastors are around people a lot, and they use a lot of our energy for dealing with people. Maybe this isn't an issue for you, but note that many pastors are introverted teaching types and not the outgoing people their congregation thinks they are or thinks they need. So, a day's worth of energy is used up on necessary phone calls and people time, and then the pastor has no resources left for the relationships that are filling and refreshing, if indeed such relationships can be made at all, based on the previous discussion. *Required* peopling uses up energy needed for *desired* peopling.

I appreciate Mr. Boers and his timeless insight. If you wish to further review his thoughts, be sure to check out the very personal article in *Psychology Today*'s winter 1991 (see the foregoing citation). In addition to these thoughts, I've added some of my own regarding the peculiarities of ministry work:

BECOMING ALL THINGS

Much like Boers's "playing the pastor" role, there is a constant relational tension as we navigate relationships and, as Paul puts it, we are "made all things to all men" (1 Corinthians 9:22). But this can be a challenge, to say the least. Dealing with the myriad of personalities and needs in the church can create quite a bit of chaos in your relational plan. Some people who befriend you are awkward because they feel convicted in your company, and others feel let down when you are human and make a mistake. Even though the pastor's role is to not worry about what everyone else thinks as we look to God, we can still feel like we are in third grade, being the odd man out by being who God wants us to be, setting that example, while others are being superficially relational and seemingly connected. This is all at risk of the success of our congregation, job, and livelihood. As a bonus, if this sounds like your actual grade school story, then it will be even more painful an experience.

SPIRITUAL ATTACKS

The spiritual attacks pastors are prone to as they lead their churches are unlike those in any other job. Yes, all of us are daily being plagued by the unseen attacks of the enemy, but it is the epicenter (or epicenters) of the system that God designed for sharing the gospel, namely, his beloved bride the church, that will take the brunt. In the movies, when a villain wants to get at the hero of the story, one of his or her greatest tools is to get to those the hero cares about most. When the villain is not stronger or more powerful or able to win in normal battle terms, he or she uses emotional and relational techniques to do as is described in John 10:10: steal, kill, and destroy. Destroy the bride, the church, and see the hero crumble is the plan. Pastors are on the front line of attacks against the bride, and they themselves, as leaders, are prone to being hunted out and destroyed to render the church ineffective in battle. There are few ways better to destroy the church than to conquer the soul of the pastor. Satan knows this. His attacks are constant and targeted and, in many cases unfortunately, effective. When one goes for the general, the queen ant, or the jugular, the system falls. And unless we as pastors accept this reality and prepare for it, we will fall prey to Satan's attacks and be destroyed. In no other job is this so prevalent, relentless, and oppressive as in the ministry. So many pastors forget this or were never taught this. They rely on their seminary degree, smarts, and processes, while failing to prepare themselves spiritually and mentally for this reality. *This* is the battle that we are fighting, not the one against the angry parent, the unsuccessful program, or the low attendance. Satan is a crafty fellow, and his strength lies in deception. He deceives us too many times by causing us to be distracted by the things around us while he destroys the innermost parts of us.

FAITH/WORK/LIFE BLUR

A significant challenge that pastors deal with is not just the work–life balance but also the blur that happens when his or her personal relationship with God becomes his or her professional relationship with God. Everything that happens is or could be a sermon illustration. Everything that happens to you is part of your professional development. And somewhere in there, you forget to have your personal quiet times; instead, it all just becomes sermon prep. Too many times, your days of rest start with a time with God, but that time with God spawns a sermon series idea or a direction to take at work with a struggling member. For the accountant, on the contrary, a day where you spend more time with God provides clarity, closeness, and a fresh perspective. If He gives you a resource to help someone or a direction in life, it's likely not about accounting. For a pastor, a day off with the Lord is a day off with your work in tow. Finding a balance between work and life is critical to maintaining healthy boundaries. And there is no easy fix. Early in my career, I was advised, in a conversation on the same matter from a senior pastor, to be adamant about the separation of the two. There is sermon prep time and it needs to stay different from personal time in prayer that is not intended for work solutions. However, God does what He does in the midst of them both, so I can't guarantee you won't get work solutions while on the personal time anyway. "Work" is everywhere. Is it safe to say that Satan can even use your disciplines to keep you wrapped up in the Lord's work while he slowly destroys you on the inside without raw personal growth and reflection? While the businessman needs to balance work and life, the minister struggles to balance work and life when life is part of his work and his work is his life.

FAMILY STYLE

One of the unique challenges that came to manifest in my world was this family-style work environment that had both benefits and detriments. Probably relatable to by anyone who works in a family business, the nuances of church life make it just a little bit more difficult to be vulnerable, so you end up in some of the loneliness traps mentioned above. In my corporate-world days, I could share a little bit if I needed to or else keep it private, and the office work was still the office work. There were professional expectations, etiquette, and rules. But in the church world, many of these churches being run by people who "just love the Lord," these rules and points of etiquette may be unestablished or misunderstood. After all, we're just like family, right? Praying for each other and taking the same liberties one might with a family member or sibling, people who work in a church environment share stories, tease each other, share things, and interact in ways that don't fit in a work environment but that can be justified in family relationships where people "really care for you." The line between appropriate and inappropriate is confusing.

I've also seen that it is difficult to move on and mature into a new role or become who God wants you to be, just as it's difficult for twenty-five-year-old, well-groomed, and professional Steve not always to be seen as "Stinky Steve" by his family members, because everyone remembers that he would never take a shower when he was young and always smelled. Being too much like family can be limiting in a person's development and pursuit of new roles and direction, especially in the family churches that have maintained long-term staffing and have very loose professional balance. Whether you think there is value in a family environment at your church is up to you. I've seen it both ways, but if family is your intent, be aware of where those boundary lines get crossed and of the dynamics that are at work.

SELF-CARE

As a therapist and a pastor, I have come to realize how many churches separate themselves and their culture from the physical needs of the body and what feels to them like not relying on God. For pastors who exist in this culture, it is challenging to find time to exercise, rest, and in general, say no. It seems that many churches are so fearful of the secular world having impact on their spiritual domain that they avoid or even reject messages of self-care beyond the Sabbath Day and the morning quiet time. They deny the fact that God designed our bodies and that our bodies need very tangible things that are not substituted by "just trust God" and "God will get you through." Pastors live in a world of "If you just had enough faith, you wouldn't need normal amounts of sleep, counseling, exercise, fun, vacations, or hobbies." More on this later.

MOTIVATION

I wonder, as we look back at our attachment chapter and our relational needs, how many people unknowingly get into ministry to solve a past problem or fuel a current fire. Are they proving or disproving something? Are they seeking or avoiding something?

How about you? If you were to be honest, where would you say your motivation is coming from? Likely you have a Jesus answer, but I would challenge you to take a deeper look at what your desires are. I would even throw out that many pastors aren't taking their time off, which we discussed earlier, because they don't want to give their hearts time to manifest their true desires. Technically, you don't capture your thoughts. You keep your thoughts captive so you don't have to hear what you are afraid of hearing. Perhaps your prayer life is hindered because you don't want a still, small voice to interrupt the mechanism you have been operating or the system you have set up and the goals you have in mind. Perhaps this is the first time you have been challenged on this. Or perhaps it's a recurring thought that you're keeping at bay.

Interestingly, the most recurring and most common needs of a human being tend to be respect and affirmation. Some of the most tangled by-products of ministry are respect and affirmation. What a perfect fit for inappropriate reasons. But the fact is that many of the ten relational needs that we crave, regardless of which ones drive you, can be satisfied in your ministerial role if you find yourself allowing it to happen. Again, it's a gut check because, on the surface, Jesus is your scripted answer.

Now, granted, many of our activities in life subconsciously are meeting these ten relational needs that we desire to have met, but the issues arise when they don't even though we "need" them to. Many times, the senior pastor, the elders, or the congregation can't meet your relational need because either they aren't equipped personally to do so or the system in place doesn't make such a thing feasible. And your pastoral role can't meet your need either. Then you continue to seek and become disappointed time and time again, and you become frustrated with your situation. Then, there's a good chance you start running. Conversely, if you are that senior guy or elder, your need for respect and order in your house can drive maladaptive behaviors. Your need to be appreciated, respected, accepted, and affirmed can become authoritarian.

In reflection of my story, I think—no, I know—that some of these things came into play in my journey. Themes that are now very clear to me played themselves out in my family of believers in a way that made my role more challenging and set up conflict with other themes that were also at play. We often forget that even though we have themes at play, others have their own wounds and experiences that may exacerbate ours, and vice versa. This dynamic makes an already challenging calling sometimes unbearable.

CHAPTER 5

RUNNING

I titled this section "Running" after the U2 hit "Running to Stand Still," which features powerful lyrics that end with the following:

> You got to cry without weeping,
> Talk without speaking,
> Scream without raising your voice.
> You know I took the poison
> From the poison stream,
> Then I floated out of here.

I liked U2—still do—but the older stuff is a powerful connection to spiritual truths and emotional awakening for me more than the newer offerings. One of the things I enjoy most is finding spiritual connections in secular music. I feel that it's one of the ways God speaks to me. So, why this song? Why these lyrics? This is my story, and this is the chapter I feared writing the most, not from an emotional standpoint but from a standpoint of helping some without hurting others. My ministry life has been a challenge for many of the same reasons all of us in ministry struggle: because it's hard and because I am front and center in a great spiritual battle, taking the bullets over and over and over again. The local church exists to share God with the world, so why wouldn't we be attacked with Satan's fullest army and his most powerful weapons? I was attacked indeed. Some of my attacks came in the form of relationship struggles, in which case I have tried to take responsibility for my part in the situation. My intent is to heal, not to harm, and now I hear story after story of pastors struggling with relational challenges and Satan using these struggles to break down the pastorate, to weaken the church, and to take Christ's bride ransom for a season—or forever, in some stories. I struggled, and I think there is value in sharing my story and other stories and what I have learned from the journey.

I want you to know that struggle does things to the body and to the mind. It's why PTSD is such an issue. It's why trauma is something that needs to be addressed. It's why I felt that I was losing my mind. It's why ministers leave the calling and pastors fall to adultery, pornography, and any of a myriad of ill-fated coping mechanisms. This is not an inclusive list of what stress and struggles do. I would recommend you read a book such as *The Body Keeps the Score*, by Bessel Van der Kolk, MD, to fully understand the effects of trauma on a person's physical body and mental aptitude.[3] I've been through it, the book and the trauma, and I concur. These are a few points relevant to my world:

WORK

The thing about church work is that it's church and work. And when work is stressful and one has a negative attitude toward work, one also has a negativity toward church, and then things get messy. When average Joes get frustrated at work or are struggling, they find comfort in God, their church relationships, and study. There's a separation of bucket filling and bucket emptying. When someone in the ministry gets in a stressful place, the answer is still to find comfort in God, but there is really no separation, and the triggers are all around. There's a claustrophobia that creeps in, and you want to step away, but you have to lean into it. You feel guilty when you just want to stop thinking about Jesus for a few days, but you know that's not right. Still, that's what you feel like doing. Or maybe you think you want to stop thinking about Jesus, but you feel in your gut it's not right, and your brain gets all jumbled, and then shame comes in just to seal the deal. How do you handle that? I think it's what many pastors deal with regularly. I think it's what drives some of them mad. How do you say you want out when you really don't? You want out of the pain and hurt that you are experiencing, but you're not sure how to make it go away. Yet in some way it's part of the suffering you signed up for, and nobody said it was going to be easy. Jesus suffered, so why don't we pastors? Then comes the accusing thought that mental health doesn't have a place in church and that if you were more spiritual, it would all be fine. And, *You're a pastor, for Pete's sake; get it together.* You ask yourself, "What else can I do?" thinking, *Maybe I'm just not cut out to be in the ministry.* Crash.

I'll admit I've exaggerated here, but not too much. It becomes hard to be as productive as you used to be or want to be. When you struggle with your work for God, going to God doesn't seem as if it's going to give you what you are looking for. This is the time to consider what it is you are really looking for. Deep down, you realize that you've messed something up along the way and have gotten your priorities and your processes out of whack, but yet there you are.

CHILDREN

Probably my greatest regret is the impact my journey had on my children. Although much of this is assumptive, I have a degree and some life lessons that give me some credibility when I say it had an ill effect on their view of the church and their need to walk with

God and rely on His sovereign provision. I trust that what Satan meant for evil, God will use to advance His kingdom someday through their exposure. It's difficult in any family to balance the exposure to real life and protection from the negative things. I do feel that there should be age-appropriate real-life exposure to prepare kids for the real world so that the kids know what is causing stress in the family. Kids have a tendency to assume it's them, or maybe it's Mom and Dad (especially depending on how the stress is manifesting), and that creates a whole different level of stress as kids don't know how to manage it all (unlike adults, who now have it all figured out). So, I really don't know if I handled it all well, but I do feel that it will be God's miracle when my children reconnect with a church body. Growing up in a generation that has begun to dismiss organized religion doesn't help their journey, but my role is to trust God in His process. I have given this matter to Him a number of times.

I also worry about what my mental absence, and in many cases my physical absence, did to my children's worldview, their needs, and the way they view God. More often than not, we can connect a person's view of God to his or her view of his or her earthly father. We can then see how the individual trusts God, loves God, or relates to God according to how he or she views his or her loving or unloving, available or unavailable, reliable or unreliable father. I fear that my son will, at best, unknowingly see God as a loving God who's there when he needs Him but will not have time for a daily relationship. I will say that by the grace of God, we have been making up for lost time in that area, so I'm happy to report that God is making progress. The sad part is that my son really doesn't need me for anything anyway; he just YouTubes it if he doesn't already know how to do something, but usually he already knows how to do it.

As powerful as the father's role is with the son, the role with the daughter is tenfold. My daughter needs to know that she is beautiful, worthy, and worth being rescued. I hope that I have given those things to her. Men often underestimate the power and importance they have in meeting the needs of their daughters. For a beautiful picture of this, read *Captivating* by Staci Eldredge.[4] I pray that my preoccupation, my stress, and my negativity toward my church work didn't drive a wedge between my daughter and her spiritual life. Stress bleeds. Anxiety bleeds. Satan makes the path.

Trauma is something that cannot be contained to a single individual. Whether it's military PTSD, the traumatic loss of a loved one (such as our friends' loss as described in the introduction), or some other life situation, trauma is systemic in nature because we are relational by design. None of us exists in a vacuum. Our lives affect our family and those around us. You may have needed to read that today. Your stress, your addiction, and your behaviors do affect others.

MY WIFE

This is starting to sound like a big apology letter—not my intent. My family knows this stuff that I'm sharing and it's been processed; I'm just sharing it to acknowledge that challenges are not experienced alone. And if you think you are handling it incognito, then know you are not. My wife likely has suffered to the greatest degree. I think the only pain worse than the pain a person experiences is the pain he or she experiences for someone else. My wife, and probably your spouse, holds the mental, physical, and relational damage too. She wears the struggle too, but she has very little control or input regarding it. She doesn't fully know what's going on in my heart or my mind. All she sees is the effects of my ministerial work and what I'm able to share. I feel that it's not fair to our spouses to be so intimately close to us yet so helplessly unable to assist. They often find themselves juggling between asking how we're doing or leaving us alone because, depending on the day, we need either empathy or avoidance. About all our spouses have available to them is prayer.

I hate it when people say all we have left to try is prayer. We have that so messed up. Somehow, we've gotten it all out of order of priority. I hope your prayer life is not like that.

The reality is, we say it because we do pray last! We say it because we are going to work hard, try again, ask around, change our method of attack, and then, if none of that works, pray about it. Sorry to be blunt, but that's messed up. I'm not even going to put a reference in here because I don't think you need me to explain why, yet we do poorly prioritize prayer, and we say it.

In many ways, it makes us feel helpless when our spouses are having difficulty because of our work in ministry. That is where my wife was, helpless to help and watching me decline. For her benefit, I will clarify that she was praying first, so when we said all she had left was prayer, she had thrown the kitchen sink at it and everything else had let her down. Prayer was "all she had left."

She did pray. I will tell you that regardless of the fact that God does hear prayers and answers them, simply knowing that someone is actively praying for you does give you strength and does help improve your perspective. It does help you see a hope that you hadn't seen before. And here's the cool thing—your faith is systemic too. You can't just be into God and not affect those around you. God used this time to help my wife work on trust and surrendering control. She's a fixer and a doer (lucky me), but she had very tangible influence. She learned to listen and love, to ask and adjust, and to trust God for rescue and redemption. In retrospect, I wish I had done better, but I trust God that it was His will and His purpose to grow us both.

LONELINESS

This one is hard. It's probably the most triggering to me now and, from what I've learned, is the most damaging and dangerous for people in ministry. Church struggles leave you isolated and lonely. No one believes this until they are in it. It seems so counterintuitive, so logically incorrect, but trust me and many others—it's real. There was a quotation I picked up some time ago; I'm sure I'll butcher the Instagram-perfect version of this, but basically it said, "Loneliness doesn't mean being alone." Now, actually being alone can be great! Jesus did it and encouraged it. I'm doing it now as I write this. But, in the words of Carl Jung, "Loneliness does not come from having no people about one, but from being unable to communicate the things that seem important to oneself, or from holding certain views which others find inadmissible."[5]

That's real loneliness. I mentioned earlier in *Scream without Raising Your Voice* that I felt that I was always the black sheep of the family. The keyword is *felt*. Our perceptions can drive our reality as we carry them from relationship to relationship, family to family, job to job. And then when we find an environment that exacerbates or seemingly affirms the perception, we solidify our beliefs and live in that reality. I really don't know if it's a true reality or not, and it's not important to know for the vision of *Scream without Raising Your Voice*, but I do know that loneliness is a painful place to be. You start to doubt your self-worth and your decisions, and mostly you start doubting the necessity of your existence. If nothing I say matters, and if I get it wrong all the time, then what am I doing? When these thoughts emerge, it is apparent that Satan has grabbed hold of the mind.

Let's consider the impact of loneliness a bit. Research out of Brigham Young University suggests that there is robust evidence showing that loneliness and social isolation increase the risk of premature death by 50 percent.[6] Loneliness is actually more of a threat to our society than the deadly obesity epidemic that has been on the front page of our newspapers for so many years. Yet we seldom talk about it. If you are suffering greatly from loneliness and social isolation, please seek help. In some cases, loneliness truly is environmental and a change of venue, a change of friends, can help. Or simply sharing your concerns with others helps. In other situations, it's a mindset that a skilled therapist or life coach can help you to turn around. Or maybe you're stuck in a pattern established by an old wound that needs to be addressed. Sometimes, it takes a dose of medication to get you back on track. Regardless, I can assure you that it won't likely go away without being addressed, even though one hopes that it will. God can do anything, but what He likes to do is bring people into our lives who can help us. We often choose to resist help for fear of looking weak or revealing our shame. Remember that loneliness kills; please reconsider if you're resistant.

HOPELESSNESS

There is one word that scares me more than *lonely*, and that's the word *hopeless*. You see, *lonely* still has an option, and that option is hope! "I hope things are better"; "This is hard, but maybe when …"; "Someday I'll …" But hopelessness extinguishes all those options. Hopelessness looks more like wandering in the neighborhood across the street from the church, not sure what your next step is because you don't have any as far as you can tell. Hopelessness is focusing on the fact that you have let your marketable business skills decline and you're so far behind the curve that there is no way you can even step out of ministry and provide for your family. Hopelessness is wondering if this would be a good time to hand your handgun over to the men in your accountability group because you just don't feel right.

You may have come to have one of these feelings. If so, you're wondering, *Why is it so hard to tell somebody I'm struggling?* I have a few thoughts:

First, it's simple pride. If your church has not established a safe place to be broken and weak, your first inclination will not be to be the first one to cry uncle. You can do it, you can make it; trust God and everything will be all right. Comparison makes us look at others and assume they are rocking and rolling, so there must be some special formula for pastors, if only you can find it. Maybe you think you should work harder. Maybe it's that you pray more, or maybe it's that you need a better accountability group. It must be something, you tell yourself.

Another reason is there could be a fear of facing the answer. It's the same reason you haven't had a physical in more than five years or had that spot on your back looked at. We don't want to have to face the reality of being broken, damaged, less than, or unable to make it through. We fear the what-ifs. We've heard stories of the previous pastors who struggled and were shipped off to rehab or a "sabbatical" and never seen again. We fear not being in control of the situation or, worse, being *seen* as not being in control of the situation.

Third, shame may play a part. Somewhere along the way, we have set up expectations that "OK" people are OK and that "not OK" people have problems. We've defined a generation of Christians by stating that if one's Bible is falling apart, then one isn't falling apart. How does that hold up to scriptural truth? Shame is perhaps one of the most powerful themes I've come across in the last few years, along with its incredible ability to isolate us. That's its job. That's how Satan uses it, and it's shutting down good people. For a powerful look into shame, you may wish to read a book I was mesmerized and deeply moved by, Dr. Curt Thompson's *Soul of Shame*,[7] which I feel is a must-read for anyone in a helping profession. He states that it's only in our willingness to share our shame with others, within a safe community, that we begin to weaken the grip of shame. By defeating its purpose to isolate, we free not only ourselves but also those who hear us share as the latter share their own stories and begin to heal. It's a contagious process of defeating the enemy, but it isn't easy, and it starts with one bold individual.

PHYSICAL

It was late in my journey when I started to feel the effects of stress on my body. If you google "the effects of stress on the …," Google will provide you an extensive list of valid answers from "body" to "brain" to "immune system" to "your heart." Thank goodness I wasn't pregnant. Stress affected me. Physically, during a season of stress, the body releases cortisol to prepare you for action. Cortisol is what we use to fight off an attacker or perform on a pop quiz. It's purposeful and powerful. The adrenal cortex manages the release of a number of other hormones designed to help us navigate life. But when we stay in stress, our bodies can't keep up with the demand of cortisol and everything gets out of whack. It affects our blood sugar levels, our immune system, and the ability to fight off inflammation, one of cortisol's primary roles. Stress kills. When your body is constantly under attack, your brain says to send all hands on deck and you get out of balance. When you are in survival mode, your body does not focus on digestion or some of the other nonsurvival skills. The sympathetic nervous system is focused on elevated breathing, releasing performance hormones, and creating acute awareness. In 2016, at the height of my stress, I began a significant battle with digestion that ultimately resulted in the removal of my gallbladder as an attempt to "solve the problem." I lost my gallbladder in this battle, but it didn't make the stress go away and it didn't markedly improve my digestion.

I've come to feel it wasn't about a failing organ; it was about my body being in a very unhealthy state of trying to deal with life. Now, as I heal, I'm adjusting to digesting without a gallbladder, which pretty much requires for me the same routine that would have kept it inside me. Ironic. Frustrating.

Perhaps most troubling for me and the most difficult to write about, for two reasons, is when I started noticing a cognitive decline in my fine motor skills. It's a scary thing to say because when this happened, I assumed the world would not find me credible or would limit how much they needed me and how much time they invested in me. At the height of my stress, I found myself stuttering or fumbling my speech. For someone who was proud of his ability to articulate and communicate orally, this quickly became a growing concern. Somewhere between the biochemical effects of stress on the brain and the psychological stress of feeling as if my efforts and answers were of no value, my ability to voice myself grew dim and unconfident. Shortly thereafter, I noticed my left-brain/right-brain dexterity was no longer tightly synchronized, and typing became a significant issue, which made self-confidence in doing any job a challenge. The stress was wearing me down mentally and physically. All this fed the hopelessness. All this fed the shame.

These aspects may be part of your story as well, or you may have other themes that need to be expressed. Pastors sit in my office with their lives and their bodies falling apart. Yours may be as well. I hate that for you. The good news is, you don't have to be hopeless and you are far from helpless regardless of what your mind and body are telling you. It's important to take a minute and reflect on that. You are also not alone. Many of us have been there, and you know—deep down you know—that God has not abandoned you even though it may feel like it. God has made us resilient and adaptable. He is fully aware of your circumstances and is walking with you through your journey. You have survived thus far. You are able to change things. There is always another option. Seek this clarity from God today. He loves you.

For strength in my running, I loved reflecting on the seventh verse of 2 Timothy, where Paul reminds Timothy that the gift God gave us is a spirit of strength, power, and love, not timidity. But in verse six, he tells him to "stir up the gift of God," so we get the picture of a small coal in the depths of our soul that is on the verge of going out and it requires stirring, blowing on, and the addition of kindling. When we see it there under the loneliness, fear, and sadness, we need to be reminded of what it is capable of. Far too often I was screaming, not stirring; running, not fanning.

CHAPTER 6

REFLECTIONS

In my darkest time, I *was* seeking God. I was longing for rescue but also longing for environmental change. I suppose I was a little schizophrenic in my prayer life, but I honestly didn't know the answer. One of the challenges with your darkest hour is not the emotional roller coaster but the emotional flat line. You see, as humans, one of our effective mechanisms to squash the emotional pain of trauma is to deny it—tell ourselves not to experience it and avoid it altogether. We "stuff it" or we "stay strong" and don't let ourselves deal with it. The danger is that we can't just flatten a single emotion. When we flatten emotions as a category, we end up flattening overall. If you close the gate to sadness, then you close the gate to joy. If you deny the hurt, the anger, and the pain, then you are training your body to deny the joy, the love, and the passion.

I see a number of men who come to me flat, depressed, and unemotional, saying to me that they can't cry or that they don't have emotions. It's typical that men in general aren't in touch with their emotions, somewhat because of the way they're designed and somewhat because of their experiences and culture growing up. Society frowns on emotional men. This isn't new information. Too many know that "men don't cry," "men are strong," men "deal with it and move on." We have a feeling chart at the office that lists feeling words so guys can get better at identifying their emotions. After years avoiding their emotions, somehow, in four sessions, we pastors are supposed to bring these men back in touch with themselves. But when we are dealing with flat lives—for example, people who don't even get emotional at their sporting events or the loss of a loved one—we find that somewhere along the way they have decided, often unconsciously, not to feel pain. In doing so, they have removed the ability to feel joy as well. Dealing with our pain allows us to experience our joy. Yes, emotions can be tricky.

EMOTIONS

I have heard it said that emotions are landmarks that help us to know where we are, not directional markers to help us know where to go. I get it. We can do some interesting things by following our gut. Scripture tells us that the way of a human's heart is deceitful:

> The heart is deceitful above all things, and desperately wicked: who can know it? (Jeremiah 17:9)

Acting on our hearts' desires can get us into trouble, and many churches stay away from emotion and feel-good messages. It is not encouraged to consider our hearts and our needs and desires. But let us also consider these verses:

> Keep thy heart with all diligence; for out of it are the issues of life. (Proverbs 4:23)

> A new heart also will I give you, and a new spirit will I put within you: and I will take away the

stony heart out of your flesh, and I will give you an heart of flesh. (Ezekiel 36:26)

Trust in the Lord with all thine heart; and lean not unto thine own understanding. (Proverbs 3:5)

We ignore the emotions of our hearts, yet it is from our hearts that the wellsprings of life are generated. It's with our hearts that we trust in God because we can't *know* everything about Him. That's what Adam and Eve tried to do. We must live by faith, and faith is *felt*. To help us do this, God has given us new hearts, ones that feel, love, and hurt and are not flat and hard like stone. So why don't we worry more about our hearts and our emotions? Keeping your heart with all vigilance is dealing with pain, loss, and hurt and not letting it eat away at you. And what's interesting about the springs of life is that they don't just give life to us. They are meant to flow into the lives of others. When we don't deal with our pain, when we flatten ourselves, we limit our ability to let life flow through us to others.

I so wanted to be rescued. I so wanted my emotions to matter and for this flattening to be gone. I often found myself in a state of numbness. I was unwilling to blink, unwilling to move my head. I was somewhere between catatonia and "the stares" as I sat in life, unsure of my next hour or my next option. I was emotionally drained, lonely, and desperate. But God was rescuing me.

WHAT WORKS

In hindsight, I look at things that worked and those that didn't work. In my journey, there were times to cry without weeping, talk without speaking, and scream without raising my voice. If *Scream without Raising Your Voice* is to be of help to others, I suppose I had better share some of the better practices. But keep in mind,

I'm still on the journey. I can tell you what has been helpful for me and speculate on other things that possibly would be beneficial. I will try to be honest with my assessments. I heard a powerful message reminding me that we often run into our dysfunctions in order to find comfort, instead of running to where God wants us. I'll confess that there are dysfunctions in my journey and my life, some of which I found to console me during my dark times. Perhaps I should mention the hit of dopamine that made me feel good. It tickled my reward center and made me keep going back.

GO TO COUNSEL

For me, I was fortunate to have godly counsel at all stages of my situation. There were some people who knew what was going on intimately and some who didn't know the people but knew the circumstances, as well as some who didn't know the circumstances but knew the people. Seeking wise and godly counsel is valuable to give you a perspective outside your emotions and your filters. This counsel can bring you to reality and guide you to scripture you may be avoiding. Let's face it: as much as we hate it when people use scripture out of context, our own brokenness can take us to the scripture that comforts, avoiding the scripture that convicts. The other thing counsel can do is to confirm you in your journey and give you a realistic grounding to substantiate the reality of what you think you are dealing with. It can be maddening if no one sees what you are seeing and if indeed your counsel denies your perspective. Then your journey may be different from the one you originally defined.

The dangers of counsel can be the dysfunction I mentioned earlier. If your counsel consists of your mother and the guys you bowl with, then you may just be seeking affirmation, not perspective. Stories like this concern me. Be aware of a habit of running to the gossip and the pat on the back because it makes you feel good, which then keeps you from seeking God's will and a biblical perspective. You also need to watch out for scope. There's a fine line between getting confirming perspectives and building an army or splitting the church.

It's best to seek counsel from an unbiased, disinterested third party so that you can work on your issues. As I write this, I realize that it's yet another reason why pastors and those in ministry have a hard time dealing with frustration and work-related problems, because it's not just a work issue. It's a church issue. It's OK to have frustrations. It's OK to have difficulties with people, but as stewards of the church, we know that often it's hard to find anyone to talk with because it may be perceived that we are stirring up trouble in the church. This is especially true if it's an issue with leadership or church direction. This is another reason we have created Perissos—to allow for pastoral counsel in unbiased arenas.

GO TO GOD

This may seem to be a no-brainer, but we often find ourselves out of whack in our thought process as we deal with trauma and some of our disciplines fall short. We suck it up, plan an attack, and try to overcome, especially as men. When it's about work that is related to church, even our relations with God can get a little jaded if we aren't careful. We can get mad at God or, worse, even become ambivalent. But the scriptures remind us, in James 1:5, that when we have no wisdom on how to handle our situation, we are to lean into Him, asking Him to guide us and give us wisdom.

> If any of you lack wisdom, let him ask of God,
> that giveth to all men liberally, and upbraideth
> not; and it shall be given him. (James 1:5)

He is adequate. He is abundant. He wants to meet you where you are. He's OK if you're mad at Him, the church, or whomever. He wants to hear it from you. He is the one person you can talk to about your weakness, your brokenness, your fear, your sin, or whatever without judgment. Because He already knows it all. We forget this too often. We, like Adam and Eve, cover ourselves with fig leaves of silence and avoid coming into contact with God because we don't want Him to know we are having a hard time working for the church. We don't want Him to know we are mad, or jealous, or scared, or lonely. "Where are you?" He asks. We reply, "I heard You in my recliner in the den in the morning, and I was afraid because I was angry [or jealous, or scared], so I avoided You." But it was God—and only God—who had a solution to the problem. He not only gave Adam and Eve a solution for the sin, He also provided a solution for their feeling of shame. He gave them a solution for their need for security and their need for value and acceptance. He met them where they were and met their physical and relational needs. Go to God.

THERAPY

Here's the deal: a lot of people, especially men, don't understand their emotions or that they have a lack. They don't care how you feel because they aren't comfortable with their own feelings, so they need to find someone who is. Typically, this is a counselor. Sometimes it's a pastor. I have been more and more surprised to find so many pastors in my conversations who are intelligent scriptural rock stars but don't relate well to people. I get it—they lead the church and run a "business," but they struggle in the area of connecting. They are using their gifts, but it leaves their staff limited unless there is another pastor to fill this role. One of the leading theological schools in the nation offers only one class on counseling over the course of its rigorous theology degree program. I find that many elders are great godly men, but they are appointed because of their business acumen or leadership skills. They can call up a scripture, but they can't call up a connection point between you and themselves and empathize or console. They can discipline and disciple but not listen and learn. I was fortunate to have some caring men in my life, but story after story—maybe your story—is that there is no one who gets it. No one relates to what you are going through because either they truly don't relate or they don't have the skill set to listen. If you were to talk to them about relational needs, they would find you weak and needy. I get it. Find a counselor.

PERSEVERANCE

My greatest tool to help with perseverance, which is second only to the daily provisions of God, is a paradigm shift. I first heard of the term *paradigm shift* when I read Stephen Covey's book *The 7 Habits of Highly Effective People*[8] years ago as a young businessman. However, the term was coined by American physicist and philosopher Thomas Kuhn years prior. Suffering, for instance, is never fun, but if you read any essay on the purpose of suffering, you will find out that there is a purpose for your suffering!

When we change our paradigm of working in the ministry, we see things differently. I will tell you here one thing that I dislike. I don't like interviewing people for church jobs, especially those people who have not yet worked in church. They come in all excited and just know that it would be heaven on earth to work for a church. They think all their stressors would go away and that life would be perfect if only they could just get hired, which would let them be that much closer to God. Even if you feel that you can warn them a little bit without throwing your church under the bus, they won't believe you. They need a change of perspective that, honestly, they can't receive because their brains cannot comprehend it based on what they have constructed as reality. Satan is hard at work in the church, and it's a battlefield of spiritual attack far beyond what is found outside the church walls.

I often use this paradigm-shifting analogy when I have people sitting in my office. When marriage is tough, or work is tough, or no work is tough, we look at it as a boot camp for whatever God has in store for the person's or people's future. For whatever special mission He is going to assign them to next year or in five years, this is the training ground. It's not about removing the struggle. It's about what the person needs to learn in this struggle to make him or her the person God wants him or her to be. In what ways does such a person struggle well, and in what areas does he or she need to grow? God likely will not make you swim in freezing water if you are good at swimming in freezing water. There's not much growth opportunity there. However, if you can't trust Him for your next paycheck, then you may find yourself in that drill, and maybe more than once. This boot camp paradigm shift sets the stage for growth and opportunity. But I get it; there may be a time to stop, but usually it's not when you think it is.

I was struggling with a significant question in my journey, and a godly man who had traveled this journey before me counseled me always to remember that when the time is right, I will know. I lived with that wisdom in my head for years because there were many times I thought I should quit, and some around me thought I should do so as well, but in my gut, I knew God wasn't done with me yet. It wasn't necessarily what *I* could do, but what *He* could do in me and through me. It was my heart that kept me in; my mind was ready to give up. Heart 1, head 0. If I got a tattoo, it would probably say "In God's Timing" because trusting in Him was the freezing water he had me swimming in for my bootcamp experience. I felt a little bit like a child in the back of an old van, bouncing around, sick to my stomach, asking, "Are we there yet? God, are we there yet?" He kept saying, "A little bit farther; it's right around the corner." Trusting Him for His provision, His plan, and His perseverance was a daily struggle for me, but He delivered as He always does. I knew it was time.

WHAT DOESN'T WORK

It's not always easy to be the best boot camp recruit, but then again, if you were good at everything, what would you have to learn? In our brokenness, and driven by unmet needs, we can encounter pitfalls and fall into maladaptive behavior patterns. I think it's important to look at failure. No, I think it's *critical* to look at failure because we have a strong tendency not to do so. Before I spill pastoral shame stories, let me talk about failure a bit. I'd like to have some conversation before we remove the fig leaf.

Failure is important, not in the way mentioned in Romans 6:1—shall I go on sinning, then, so that God's grace may increase?—but by the simple act of trying something and then learning from it if we fail. Let's go back to my office and any number of young men who are trying to "adult" whom the world has frozen in fear of failure. Why? Because they don't know how to recover. They have never gone through this, and they have no confidence that they can go through it. *What if I fail?* Eduardo Briceño, in a TED talk entitled "How to Get Better at the Things You Care About,"[9] shared with me (and the world) that one reason we see this struggle in our up-and-coming generation is the way we have structured learning. He says that there is a performance zone and a learning zone. It's in the learning zone where we are free to explore, try new things, and fail. Failure gives us confidence and the ability to recover. We have structured our education system, however, so that we study, listen, and then perform, that is, take the test. We are teaching to the test rather than teaching to learn. As an additional perspective, it seems that social media has two options. You either have a huge number of followers or you fail. And if you fail, you end up being on the fail video. So, if you're sort of good or not good yet, you'd better not try or else there's a good chance for public humiliation or shame. We are living in an all-or-nothing culture, and many young adults are stuck in nothing. We don't know how to fail because it's not safe to fail.

The local radio station often plays little snippets of wisdom. I apologize that I'm not sure who said this (I hope to get an answer before this goes to press, but if not, know that it was a Christian comedian; this is not to be accredited to me), but someone said to imagine that you try something new every year. For instance, what if every Easter you baked a new dish? I liked where he was going with this. Try something new once a year. Good call. But then I had a perspective shift. He went on to ask, what if you were to fail at making that new dish? You would have 364 days to sit in that failure and let it stew, let it become a memory, let it become a potential family joke or stigma. But what if you were to try something new once a week? Six days isn't too long a time to sit in a failure. It's just enough time to learn what you did wrong so you can do it better the next time. We need to try things. We need to learn to recover. We need to fail. Let's get back to failure stories now that I've told you how awesome it is to fail.

It's been said that having some time away gives you some clarity, but I also think it allows you to forget some things— things that were hard to hold and process, things that were painful and hurtful. Time gives you that separation. I think of an abused woman who leaves her husband; after a while she begins to remember the things she misses. She sees a house for comfort, a paycheck for provision, and an "intimacy" she longs for. Her description of her previous situation becomes skewed and unbalanced. She sees the social media version, not the real version, and she starts to believe she was wrong. So, after experiencing this separation myself, I'm not sure if it's clarity or confusion, but it's another good reason to have counsel and community, for support and clarity. In spite of that concern, I have a few things to share that have shown to be ineffective in my story, as well in the stories of others as I've collaborated with them in processing their journeys.

PRIDE

It's easy to say the word *pride* during any male discussion; it's there if you look, but it's hard to look at the real issues of pride in us. Standing firm in our position, unwilling to budge or hear another position, not apologizing or admitting wrong—all these manifestations of pride stand against the efforts of restitution. We cross over a line where even if we're wrong, now we're just fighting for ourselves because we don't want to admit we're wrong. Pride can be both the start of the problem and the roadblock to resolution. Regardless of what position you hold in your mind, the cause or the victim, consider ruthlessly where pride has come into play. I have counseled pastors (and nonpastors) through pride issues in their lives, and I admit I have manifested these issues as well. I have fought against pride issues manifested in other pastors also. I can tell you that in all these cases, there truly are no winners. Having typed this, I feel compelled to clarify that pride is not the same as boundaries. Protecting yourself and your family is OK. Having boundaries means you are standing firm for good reasons. But digging your heels in because you *just know* that the church needs a third service, a balcony, or a missions van may be worth a little soul-searching as to why this is so important to you.

PERSONAL NEEDS

As I've said earlier in *Scream without Raising Your Voice*, trying to lay the foundation, our needs and desires are lying under the surface of all our relationships and stressors. We must be aware of their propensity to affect our behaviors. In many of our postmortem pastoral conversations dealing with relational conflicts, I hear about the brokenness of relationships and the need for acceptance and attention from both sides. I also discern the need for authority, the need for acceptance, and the need for someone to listen and understand. Unfortunately, seeking that your needs be met by sources that cannot provide those needs will be a fruitless and frustrating journey that always leaves you empty-handed. The more the other person "should" in your mind, the more frustrated and bitter you become. If you remember from back in chapter 2, our relational needs descriptors were clarified to state that all these needs are available through Christ. It's the only fail-safe way of getting what you need. If you happen to have a boss or employee who meets those needs, then that's a blessing, but expecting an employee to respect you when he or she didn't respect his or her father or was never respected himself or herself will be a tall order. Wanting attention from an inattentive elder board will leave you in a depleted state. Connecting the two, many of our pride issues come from an overwhelming unmet need or open wound.

I think for both of these, it's important to create an environment where we understand each other's wounds, at least to a general degree. You can do DiSC assessments or an enneagram assessment to understand relational dynamics, but until you understand a person's wounds and his or her unmet needs, you really don't know with whom you are relating. You have the presentation version of the person while the person struggles with his or her real self. Therefore, it's important for a church staff to have social relationships and to encourage vulnerability as much as you reasonably can based on your staff dynamic. Whatever your ultimate result is, the mindset should be that it is a sought-out commodity, not something to be avoided. Vulnerability breeds authenticity and intimacy. Most importantly, it starts from the top down. In most environments, you'll find the following dynamic:

It's not very difficult for a third- or fourth-tier ministry staff to be weak and share their brokenness because, as far as their position goes, they don't have much expectation placed on them. As you climb the ladder, you'll find it more and more difficult to be weak and vulnerable. There is this unwritten expectation saying that if you were spiritual enough, or if you hired the right guy, or if you knew what you were doing, you would be OK. There's no room for weakness in the very church that acknowledges that everyone is weak and broken under Christ. This is also why I believe that we end up with churches that worship their pastors more than they worship God. We must *be* broken so that God receives the focus, not us.

I'm mentally taken back to a painful message from Peter Hiett, the senior pastor of the Sanctuary Church in Denver, Colorado, as he presented his powerful message on the topic "Abundance of Poverty."[10] Plagued with the question of "How are you going to feed My sheep?" many a pastor has fallen. Hiett shared a personal account of a pastor who was struggling, and when it was suggested by a friend to speak to the elders, the pastor said, "I've seen what they do with the weak; I'll be crucified." Sad account indeed. We don't know if this is true or not of the elders, but we're reminded that perception is reality, so our reality needs to be very convincing.

PASSIVE RESCUE WISH

This was a new term for me—*passive rescue wish.* I was sitting in my fourth boundaries class that I'd been a part of teaching over the last few years, and it hit me for the first time—passive rescue wish. This was me and others. I was an open book emotionally. I'd sit in staff meetings, openly frustrated, and assume—no, expect—that someone would be concerned about why. I wanted someone to deal with the issue and resolve the problem. I wanted to matter in a way that said, *Hey! Look at Jody! There's something wrong, and we should care.*

At the same time, I want to make sure you don't hear me say, "Fake it and play like everything is OK." We have way too much of that going on in the church today. But our boundary violations or transgressions need to be expressed and communicated as we are directed in Matthew 18. Even though the need for comfort and attention is real, there's no place for a passive rescue wish in the church. If this is you, as it is others I've talked to, I would encourage you to speak up, even if you think you know nothing good will come of it.

Also consider checking out your motives and look at your needs and your attachment style. Did you have issues as a child in that you were undervalued, unheard, or bullied? Or maybe you were overheard, overvalued, and unsure how to handle someone else's opinion. I think we all have a desire to be rescued when we are struggling, but this isn't the way to wave your arms and signal the SOS for the rescue crew. The only One who can really rescue you is already fully aware of what's going on.

BUILDING AN ARMY

What does a man or woman do when he or she feels lonely and all alone? He or she starts to build an army. Seeking allegiance and confirming your perspective is one of those dysfunctions that a person can be easily roped into. It feels good to have people who see things the way we do. It takes the edge off the isolating and lonely thoughts. It affirms us (likely one of your needs as well), and it builds the community that fights the isolation you're feeling elsewhere. But it isn't healthy, even if you are 100 percent right, whatever that means.

I had a pastor talk about David and his band of outcasts and how God had brought them together. They were lonely, but they were valued and were suffering for good reason in the caves. You might find a lot of parallel in this story. God may indeed be surrounding you with people who understand and are suffering alongside you, but take a minute and check your motives to make sure you aren't building an army. Make sure it's the community that God is providing.

SILENCE

Maybe this is the passive rescue wish again, but I think it differs in that some people suffer in silence and do what they can not to show their emotional pain, not to rock the boat, and just carry on. Absolutely God can change things, and rescue can come without your doing anything beyond praying and having perseverance, but too often, silence is seen as acceptance or assumption that boundary violations aren't existent and behaviors are acceptable. Depending on what your situation is, you have to consider the instruction in Matthew 18, which specifically tells us to call out a brother or sister who has offended us. Not to slander, or gossip, or spite, but to confront with love. We are commissioned to speak truth and grace. Silence is actually part of the systemic failure that got Adam and Eve into trouble. I am amazed at people in ministry who are legitimately being abused, emotionally or physically, and are told to not say anything or that it's no big deal. I think in many ways the church is paying the price for that now, in 2021, as exposure is starting to happen and the church is finding it harder to be trusted and to gain followers and respect.

Who of us, when hearing of a friend outside the church dealing with an abusive spouse, would instruct the person to stay quiet and deal with it? Or maybe we find out that a loved one has been violated emotionally or physically. Would we tell him or her to suck it up and deal with it, to stay quiet, and not to rock the boat? Yet in some churches, it seems to be the mantra that if one speaks up, then this tarnishes God's reputation by revealing the abuse and the wrongdoing of "His people." We must call this out and find healthy, authentic healing in our churches.

I'm sure there are many more things that don't work to help you in your struggle. The list of things not to do, in reality, is infinite. I'm always amazed at how our stories can be so similar but also that we have such uniquely bizarre paths. You may have a very good understanding right now, if you are experiencing struggles in your ministry, of what isn't working for you, but you are hanging onto that behavior or choice for dear life. What is your fear? What is that thing you need so much? Whom can you talk to? I don't know where you are in your journey—if you are reading this chapter as describing the past or the present, or maybe a fearful future. If you are in the present looking at rescue ahead of you, I would challenge you to make sure that you are able to say, "I did what God asked me to do. I was the best boot camp participant I could be. I wasn't perfect, but my goal was to do what my Teacher wanted me to do so I could learn and grow and make a positive impact in the kingdom."

I have personally learned that when the conflict, stressor, or trauma is over, your most comforting feeling is knowing that you did the best you could do with what you had. When we trust in God's statutes and His direction, we find joy.

CHAPTER 7

RESCUE

'Cause I know a land called
the land of the living.
It's the world beyond those curtains
where we learned to play.
I hear the voices of my childhood singing.
It's the world beyond those doorways
where we used to play.
But you can't be an old fire if you
are burning with a new flame.
So remember that you are
never a forgotten name.

—Roo Panes

This song moves me. I feel that it is a gift from God. I like looking for gifts from God because I think we too often take the world for granted. We assume gifts from God come only in the form of healing from cancer, or making it home safe, or God's providing a job when we are unemployed. Sure, those count too, but when God tickles your heart, makes you come alive, or gives you a feeling of value that cause you to tear up, those things are also precious.

Rescue was about a land beyond the curtains. It was about a land where I could live and where I could sing unabashedly like when I was a child, unencumbered, unconcerned—a place where I used to play. He was rescuing me.

Is it time, Lord? There is a common axiom that tells us to keep going because the breakthrough is just over the hill or just around the bend. Before we had GPS on our phones, it was natural to think we had gone far enough and turn around, only to find out that we were almost there before we backed out of the mission. I think I had made an agreement with myself, again to use an Eldredge term, that I always quit too soon. I gave up too easily. I thought that I needed to see it through and finish what I had started, but God had other plans. The three-legged stool was about to be built.

> Then David the king stood up upon his feet, and said, Hear me, my brethren, and my people: As for me, I had in mine heart to build an house of rest for the ark of the covenant of the Lord, and for the footstool of our God, and had made ready for the building: But God said unto me, Thou shalt not build an house for my name, because thou hast been a man of war, and hast shed blood. (1 Chronicles 28:2–3)

A devotional was shared in my supervision/staff meeting, and I felt God saying, "Are you listening?" It was as if I had been waiting the whole time for permission from Him to leave. I had heard it, but not from Him. But I would know when it was time, according to my counsel. I so feared making a mistake, reacting out of weakness or emotion. But then He asked, "What if finishing well means not finishing?"[11] This was the name of the Priscilla Shier devotion that was read, and the ensuing revealing discussion about David communicated that even though he had planned and worked hard and determined himself to build the temple, it was God's plan for Solomon to build it. It would be called Solomon's temple with Solomon getting all the credit. But that was God's will. Sometimes finishing well is getting out of the way to let someone else take the baton. It was good for all of us at my meeting to hear, but I don't think anyone understood why I was near tears. It was great for me to hear. Leg one.

But how do I get out of the way? And to where will I go? I heard Him, but there was no clear direction. Until there was. That was where Perissos was born. *Perissos* is the Greek word for "abundant," and John 10:10 says that He came so that we might have life and have it abundantly—an exceedingly, surpassing, extravagant life. Part of trauma mastery is finding a way to give purpose to your trauma in hopes that the same thing that happened to you doesn't happen to others. So, a ministry was born. An invitation to lead this ministry was extended to me, and things started falling into place. Leg two.

Then my wife's job changed, which improved our situation, in contrast to our original plan. Insurance was provided and sponsorship was secured. The rescue began. Leg three.

The chorus played:

> I was born to be free. You were born to free me.
> I was born to be free. You were born to free me.
> I was born to be free. You were born to free me.
> I was born to be free. You were born to free me.

(Roo Panes, "Land of the Living")

BEST OF TIMES, WORST OF TIMES

Sometimes analogies aren't perfect, so take this with a grain of salt: the wandering in the desert began. When we seek rescue from a situation, whether it be an abusive marriage, a season of unemployment, a painful breakup, or a season of grief and loss, that rescue is often not what we would expect or desire when it's granted. There's often pain in the joy, and confusion in the confidence, as we navigate this new world. I'm reminded that the children of Israel weren't rescued to the Promised Land; they were rescued from Egypt. There was still a very faithful, painful journey ahead with lessons to be learned. Manna was to be provided and promises to be shared. But just as God was with the children of Israel, he will meet you in your journey as well.

Rescue can be lonely. If your rescue is a separation of sorts, it can be like leaving a town or a relationship. Friends are lost, and creature comforts are no more. I'm sitting with a man now who has all his identity wrapped up in years of work and now he has no work as far as he can tell. He's in a different town and has a different role than the one he had before, one in which he's not very comfortable. Not only does he not have his identity, but also he is not getting his need for affirmation, value, and acceptance met. If you remember from chapters 4 and 5, loneliness is a very scary place. So be careful. Find counsel, find connection, and lean into God. This need for value and identity reminds me of the Stockholm syndrome,[12] a psychological condition coined in 1973 when prisoners developed a bond with their captors because the captors fed them and "cared for" them. Like a battered wife who finds comfort in the fact that at least she knows how to play the game and where to expect the blows to come from, some of the children of Israel wanted to go back to Egypt because the rescue wasn't what they thought it should be. It didn't make sense. They became tired, frustrated, and self-righteous. We gain a sense of control in a situation like this one, albeit an unhealthy one. That need for control can send us back or drive us mad. There is little control in the desert. So again, here's a reference to a message I heard that put things in perspective for me. I was reminded of Charles Dickens's *A Tale of Two Cities*[13] and the phrase "It was the best of times; it was the worst of times." This can be what rescue looks like. We must be willing to endure great pain to achieve great freedom. I'm reminded of the scenes from war movies, or maybe being in an abusive relationship. Getting out alive can be difficult.

As counselors, our team serves a community dedicated to the rescue and rejuvenation of women who are fleeing from domestic violence. It can be the best thing they have ever done, yet they often have no resources, no skills, and no connections. It's not hard to see how difficult it really is. It's both the best of times and the worst of times for many of these women. The children of Israel wandered in the desert; women fleeing violence often sleep in their cars or beg for money, leaving many of their belongings behind. I also think of the people we see in the news who are caught in the middle of a flood and have to be rescued. They are taken by a helicopter, dangling on a wire or in the arms of a rescuer, through the floodwaters. Being rescued is not easy or fun—it's scary. Often, it's only when you are fully rescued and safe that you can find the energy to rejoice.

SOMETIMES THE RESCUE IS WITHIN

The phrase "internal locus of control versus external locus of control" was originally coined in the 1950s by Julian Rotter.[14] This tells us that a person's locus of control is a look at how much control he or she feels he or she has over his or her circumstances. An internal locus means that the person feels he or she has control over his or her circumstances; an external locus means the person feels there is a force or situation affecting and impacting his or her life. This is one of the conversations we have with clients as we assess their perspective of what is affecting their lives from the outside and what they have control over. Many times, the answer is external blame and situational focus on the struggles of life.

Many times this is a valid answer. There's a good chance that we can all assess our stories and share situations where a circumstance has created a challenge or impasse in our lives. In the ministry, it could be elders who are creating a toxic environment by their leadership or lack thereof, or simply a difficult boss. Maybe it's a process or a culture, but there are always external forces impacting us. We'd be remiss not to note that God Himself is an external (and in many ways internal) source of control or direction. There's also a good chance that our prayers of rescue revolve around the removal of ourselves from the impact of those external things. It could be freedom from a nagging wife, freedom from a job, or freedom from an addiction. *Lord, just get me out of here!*

Sometimes, the rescue doesn't work like that. God does what's best for us—for our growth and our development—and sometimes the rescue is within. Really? It's easy for us to want an escape, to get as far away from our issue, from the problem, as we can. I just had a conversation this afternoon with a guy who is struggling at his job, not a ministry job, but a job nonetheless. It's tough. He doesn't feel valued. He got a poor review. He's on a dead-end project that seems to be the proverbial thorn in his side. Therefore, he's frustrated, ready to leave, and done with it. I asked what God had been working with him on and what he had asked for in his prayer time. It turns out that his journey is to find value outside of performance and to feel valued by God and worthy of sonship.

Interesting! Here we have a guy who prides himself on hard work and success, and he's struggling at work in the areas of value, success, and a connection with a loving father. It became evident that perhaps God was using his work environment to build a perfect training ground to find value in God alone, outside of performance. I've heard it said that when we ask God for something, He's not going to give it to us; He's going to create the environment for it to happen. If we desire to learn to depend on God, He might take away what we are depending on. If we want to love people more, He may just connect us with some unlovable people.

God will use our adverse situation as a way to grow us into who He wants us to be. Pain, suffering, struggle—these are all important to experience when God wants us to go through them. Sometimes changing the perspective to see things as an in vivo lab, where we will learn valuable lessons and growth, provides a healthier view and an internal rescue. I can't help but think of a navy SEAL, or any military person as far as I'm concerned, finding success in the military but being rescued from boot camp. It was a necessary part of their journey to become who the military needed them to be. From athletes to students to everyday people, escaping the issue isn't always the answer if the struggles are meant to grow you and shape you.

That's not the only way our perspective can be changed though. We need to get into a humble pose for this section to see that there's an even more powerful paradigm shift than the one just discussed that will cause us to see things differently. What if you have been looking at the situation wrong? What? Yep, maybe your pride, your insecurity, your fear, or just your buddy Satan was creating a skewed view of reality. What if you were too scared to face the assumed embarrassment of failure, so you blamed the culture? What if you're too prideful to hear feedback, so you blame your employee or staff? What if the issue is one you have created as a means to meet a need in your life or to avoid an unmet need? We make mistakes; we are motivated by sinful motives. We have to consider this option. Yes, the culture, or your story, or the pressures can influence this, but what we are talking about here is an internal locus of control. What have you done to create this situation?

In a marriage (or in any relationship), we talk about the fact that both partners have contributed to the state of the union and thus to the problem. The proverbial tango that it takes two to perform comes to mind. It's worth considering this dynamic in whatever situation you are being rescued from. Perhaps you have 10 percent contribution, or perhaps God is trying to tell you that you've made a 90 percent impact on this situation. Rescue can still be had, but it comes with what sometimes may feel to be impossible feats. God loves this kind of rescue because it involves character change and restored relationships. Whatever the process is for your rescue here, it begins with obedience to the Holy Spirit's guidance.

> He that covereth his sins shall not prosper: but whoso confesseth and forsaketh them shall have mercy. (Proverbs 28:13)

If you have prayed for rescue here or asked God to reveal any areas of concern within you, then you've likely been prompted with a directive to forgive, admit, confess, love, or pray, or any of the myriad things that God knows will be challenging but powerful. But it may simply be to listen, care, connect, or do it differently next time, or however He wants to orchestrate this rescue. Sometimes rescue comes from within.

WHEN IT'S NOT WHAT WE WANTED

Have you ever been rescued and it wasn't quite what you wanted? You've been praying for months or years, and then it happens— but, you ask, "What is this?" Separate from just wandering in the desert, God's plan sometimes is so different from ours that it doesn't even seem like a rescue. It can feel like a failed attempt.

God works at a different level than we do. Isaiah 55:8–9 reminds us of this reality:

> For my thoughts are not your thoughts, neither are your ways my ways, saith the Lord. For as the

heavens are higher than the earth, so are my ways higher than your ways, and my thoughts than your thoughts.

We do such a good job of creating a plan for God to follow that we don't understand why He doesn't just do what we suggested and prayed for, because then everything would be great! We would be good. He would get the glory. Why doesn't God just do it right? I'm reminded of the first responder rescuers who come to our potential rescue and give us a set of directives, such as "Sit here"; "Hold on here"; or "When I say jump, jump"—or whatever the case may be. These men and women are trained in areas we aren't. They know the big picture, so we instinctively trust their words and do what they say. They know the speed of the rapids, or the location of the fire, or the potential for crossfire. God has the big picture too. Like the first responders, God needs us to trust Him and do what He says. I think somehow we get lost between "God will hear my prayers and give me what I ask" and "I know God may do something I don't understand, so I will trust Him." We believe in both, but we often bet on the first one. Like children, we think that we know what's best for us. It could be that you asked to be taken out of band or off a team, when your parents knew that rescue needed to come from the inside; or maybe you were rescued to another sport or activity, but not the one that the bad-influence teammate was a part of or the one with the apathetic leader or teacher. We can see that stuff doesn't matter to a kid seeking his or her own desire and immediate goals, but it does matter to a loving father seeking the best for his child, with long-reaching impact and vision. Sometimes rescue isn't what you planned for or even what you wanted, but that's OK if you trust that God loves you and is grooming you for the work that he has planned for you.

WHEN IT'S NOT COMING IN TIME

But how long does one wait? "You'll know when it's time," I was told by a mentor. And he was right. It seemed like forever, but in retrospect, it was very obvious why the takeoff on the runway at the airport was delayed. There was refueling to do, deicing to be done, and preparation of the runway still on the list. There were things to learn; there was growth to happen; there was perspective to gain. It was not coming in my time (or my wife's), but that was OK because it is not my time that is most important here. If you find yourself in this situation, I would encourage you to lean in and see what you can learn, trust that there's a reason for delay, and treat the situation like you would any other challenge or trial that may come your way.

Also, consider that you may be avoiding the rescue. Don't get mad at me, just consider it. I'm reminded of the old joke of the man on the roof, escaping a flood, who prays for God to rescue him. After a few minutes, a rowboat comes by and the rowers ask him if he needs help. He replies, "No, thanks. I have prayed for God to rescue me. He will hear my prayers and take care of me." A few minutes later, a helicopter comes by and asks if he needs help. He replies, "No, thanks. I have prayed to God to rescue me. He will hear me and take care of me." A few minutes later, a guy on a Jet Ski comes by. He also asks if the man needs help. The stranded man replies, "No, thanks. I have prayed for God to rescue me. He will hear my prayers and take care of me." The water rises, and sure enough, the guy ends up drowning. But he's a believer, so he goes to heaven. When he sees God and he asks Him, "Lord, I was stuck on that roof and You heard me praying! Why didn't You rescue me?" God, looking at him with the expression an exasperated father gives a child, says, "Son, I sent a boat, a helicopter, and a Jet Ski. What more do you want?"

Apparently, the man had in his mind an idea of what the rescue should look like, so for him it took too long, even to the point of his death. What if God is providing a rescue that doesn't match up to your expectations? Sometimes we get stuck on the thought that what He is providing isn't where we want to be, but we forget that a path has many steps and fail to consider that we may just be on the first one. It's important to acknowledge that the location of this unexpected rescue may just be where God wants you now, not always. Perhaps it's more of a refuge than a rescue. Perhaps there's a contact to make or a lesson to be learned. Paul ended up where God wanted him, not where Paul himself often planned to go. We see this in Acts 16:6–10:

> Now when they had gone throughout Phrygia and the region of Galatia, and were forbidden of the Holy Ghost to preach the word in Asia, after they were come to Mysia, they assayed to go into Bithynia: but the Spirit suffered them not. And they passing by Mysia came down to Troas. And a vision appeared to Paul in the night; There stood a man of Macedonia, and prayed him, saying, Come over into Macedonia, and help us. And after he had seen the vision, immediately we endeavoured to go into Macedonia, assuredly gathering that the Lord had called us for to preach the gospel unto them.

Paul had a plan, and it was thwarted. He obeyed. Maybe your rescue is taking a long time, not because of God, but because you have not surrendered your plan and heard the Holy Spirit telling you His plan. Maybe.

PART III

FUTURE

CHAPTER 8

REPAIR

After rescue comes repair. As of the writing of *Scream without Raising Your Voice*, repair is under way. There are things we don't see when we are deep in the forest. There are things others tell us that we don't believe, see, or comprehend. Your focus is often on surviving, not on growing, training, or relaxing. It's the constant flow of cortisol to help you stay afloat. It's the comfort of unhealthy coping mechanisms to try to help you find some joy. But when you are out of the abusive situation, or away from the bad news, or at the end of the season, you come out battered, damaged, and in need of repair. I had a wise friend once tell me that even when you are rescued, like a broken arm set in a cast, you will need time for healing. So true. Putting on the cast or identifying the problem doesn't make you healthy; it simply identifies a starting point. Healing from trauma requires work. And rest. Let's look at a few parts of repair.

THE MIND

Trauma affects the mind most of all. Many folks don't fully understand this. It's often not understood if you experience it, and it's definitely not understood by those around us unless they are trained in trauma awareness. I'm reminded of the great Bob Newhart skit on Mad TV with Mo Collins, where she comes to see Newhart as a psychiatrist. His solution for her anxiety is "*Stop it!*" That's the way the world outside of mental health often looks at mental health. Their solution is to stop thinking that way, get over it, move on. But it doesn't work that way. A broken mind is a critical thing to repair and dangerous to leave alone. Mental health issues are becoming more and more prevalent in our society and are being blamed for everything from the growing number of shooting sprees to homelessness, yet we as a society continue to ignore the significance of mental health. Only now are we beginning to see glimpses of conversation in Congress, and only then if we are looking for these glimpses. But what society does, doesn't have to impact your own healing and fortitude. This is a choice you make.

Romans 12:2 reminds us:

> And be not conformed to this world: but be ye transformed by the renewing of your mind, that ye may prove what is that good, and acceptable, and perfect, will of God.

Part of our healing is the renewal of our minds. Remember that Philippians 4:8 tells us how to do this:

> Finally, brethren, whatsoever things are true, whatsoever things are honest, whatsoever things are just, whatsoever things are pure, whatsoever things are lovely, whatsoever things are of good report; if there be any virtue, and if there be any praise, think on these things.

When we are in a traumatic situation, as much as we try to find the good or redefine the paradigm, we can't help but have a large focus on the pain, the fear, the damage, or the problems. A rescue can be a fresh start to the renewing of the mind.

NEW FRIENDS

Sometimes, depending on your situation, you may find it hard to believe that there are people out there who understand. There really are. It's hard to imagine that there are people out there who don't need to have an opinion, one way or the other, on your stressful situation because they like you without any exposure to or awareness of your situation. There are. These are the healthiest friends in time of repair because they pull you farther out of the forest. We live in a certain terrain for so long, cutting down trees perhaps, and we forget that there are other forests and other trees. There are marshlands and prairie lands and all sorts of people who are healthy to be around whom we would never have met had we stayed. We live in our bubbles, and even though the bubble starts to fill with constrictive gases, making it hard to breathe, we keep waving our arms around, thinking we can make it in the bubble. Sometimes it's good to pop the bubble. This thought is especially hard to take if you've lived in the same bubble for years. My generation (that just made me sound old) is the last of the people who found value in working at one place for as many years as possible. Perhaps this younger generation is more comfortable popping bubbles.

I have friends from high school, but not close friends. We live in the same neighborhood and we cross paths now and again, but we are not what I would call close. My close friends, the ones I can tell anything to, are friends I have known for twenty years or less, and all tend to exist in the same bubble. As a matter of fact, as a pastor, you may easily find most of your friendships existing in one bubble—a bubble you are afraid to pop or let air out of, even if it needs to be bled. Remember chapter 4 and the argument that a pastor's job uses up his or her social energy? Depending on what kind of personality God has blessed you with, this can hold true for sure. We have only a limited amount of energy to be used for socializing and being with others. If you are more introverted, it can be significantly less than the average person. As pastors, we are expected to engage in a certain amount of job-related socialization, to be friendly, and to chitchat. We are called to care for, care about, and concern ourselves with others daily, so much so that we have little room to invest in friendships outside the church, outside our expected amount of socialization, so we are lacking in other friendships and relationships. As a result, it's easy to find a pastor who needs to get away, be alone, and decompress. Making friends is not on the agenda. The fact that it's not on the agenda is a shame when you consider Jesus's goal to associate with the taxpayers, the sinners, and those outside the church bubble. We pastors simply are missing the point if we are falling into this trap of social exhaustion.

And that's why rescue involves new friends. New connections can bring life to a person who feels lonely, misunderstood, and dry. We fight very hard against losing friends and our connections, but we see over and over again in scripture that new connections are what God uses to carry forth His plan. Ruth meets Boaz, David meets Jonathan, and Nicodemus steps out of his religious bubble to meet Jesus.

I especially like the story of Paul and Barnabas that we pick up in Acts 15:36–40:

> And some days after Paul said unto Barnabas, Let us go again and visit our brethren in every city where we have preached the word of the Lord, and see how they do. And Barnabas determined to take with them John, whose surname was Mark. But Paul thought not good to take him with them, who departed from them from Pamphylia, and went

not with them to the work. And the contention was so sharp between them, that they departed asunder one from the other: and so Barnabas took Mark, and sailed unto Cyprus; And Paul chose Silas, and departed, being recommended by the brethren unto the grace of God.

Acts 13–14, and most of Acts 15 talks about the ministry that Paul and Barnabas were doing together. They had a tight bubble, but we see in verse 36 of chapter 15 that they split apart and made new friends. Both continued ministry, and God had plans for Paul to meet up with Timothy, which made a huge impact on his ministry and the early churches. This verse is a powerful message for me as I begin new ministries and look forward to whom God will bring into my life and what He will do through new friends and new relationships.

Something else I've learned is that friends don't leave if you pop the bubble. That's what makes them friends. Some dynamics may change, and some logistics get challenging, but these people reach out. They care, and you stay friends. Some of that is also your responsibility. Don't make the mistake of forgetting to call these people to show them that you still consider them friends even though your environment has changed. We tend to wallow a bit in our transition, and we think (hope) others will reach out to us. Don't get caught up in this lie. Friendship is a two-way street, so you're just as responsible for keeping the relationship alive if it's meant to be. Don't use your absence and the other person's urgency (or lack thereof) to contact you as a barometer to show how good of a friend he or she is. Even the best of friends sometimes fail when it comes to having good intentions.

This is honestly an area that I have struggled in as I have been one to keep friendship plates spinning, so to speak. One of my agreements that I have lived with is a belief that I have to regularly call, text, or encourage people in order to keep them active on my friend list. This alone can be an exhausting agreement. Socially, as a pastor connected to a larger than normal group of people, I find the task to be overwhelming and guilt producing of continually going through contact lists and sending texts or reengaging conversation just so I don't grow stale in the eyes of my friends. Ironically, gaining new friends has helped me in this area as it forced me to reevaluate this agreement and seek perspective from a mentor on what I should expect out of relationships and what *he* expected out of a relationship.

But maybe your rescue didn't require you to pop the bubble or even bleed it a little bit. Maybe your rescue came from within, either from within yourself or within your environment. My bet is that God used connections with new people and new relationships to change a perspective or change the environment. My bet is that God used people. He likes to use people. That's one of the reasons pastors struggle. Because of our job and because of our roles, we may find ourselves feeling isolated and thinking that we have no one to talk to. Trust me when I say that there are new friends to be found to widen your perspective and add a layer of health to your self-care plan. God uses community. And if you find yourself having to leave community, God will arrange for more to come along and shore you up. That's part of the rescue.

SIMPLE THINGS

Part of my repair is to regain a perspective on God and enjoy His simple blessings as well as His grand ones. Answered prayers are great, but so are butterflies and sunsets. As I sit here now, writing, I see that the sun is setting into a cloud display that is forecasted to bring a week of storms. It's a comfortable seventy-four degrees on the patio of a Whole Foods Market in Texas. These things have all been here for years, but it's in the repair that God has heightened my senses and reminds me that He is the Maker of all things big and small. I'm disappointed because what I thought was the kitchen of a local restaurant sending me well-wishes through aromatic smoke signals turned out to be the Fruity Pebbles and Captain Crunch blended flavoring of the young woman's vape as she sits with her boyfriend on the bench across the patio from me. She has since left the area, as did my aromatic blessing. But I noticed it. I sat in it and enjoyed it as I took in the environment around me. God blesses us daily, but we are often too tired, busy, angry, or (fill in the blank) to experience it. Rescue can be a time of reconnecting with God in a pure and a simple way like a child.

> But Jesus said, Suffer little children, and forbid them not, to come unto me: for of such is the kingdom of heaven. And he laid his hands on them, and departed thence. (Matthew 19:14–15)

We can make ministry convoluted with our programs and seven-step processes of salvation and discipleship, but in doing so we often forget the simple things. We forget to wonder in our Savior and notice Him. Our Christian life is about worshipping our God. That's why we were created, to worship Him and to introduce others to Him, so they will worship Him like children, amazed at all He does and did and excited about the next time we will get to see Him and talk to Him. Have the demands of ministry stripped you of this wonder? I remember when I was a kid and my parents were both in education. They held various roles, and for one season, my father was the principal of an elementary school. Sometimes he would go to work on the weekend to get a few things done, and sometimes he asked me and my siblings to go with him (or maybe he had to take us, but I'll choose to believe he wanted to ask us). I was pumped. I was proud of what my dad's work was, and I was pleased to be invited to be part of his work. As a child, like most adults in the kingdom, I often ran around the building like a chicken with its head cut off, not doing a thing my father asked me to do. It was so cool being there with him. The building was huge, and I got to experience the special access and the freedom, as well as the authority, because I knew him. It was the wonder of things other people either didn't have permission to see or that they saw every day and didn't find exciting at all. I saw the wonder.

On the other side of that, I worked at BNSF Railway for a number of years. A little piece of trivia that many people don't know is that the railroad is one of the largest holders of collectible art in the world. Back in the day, artists were commissioned to paint pictures of the region the train served, and then these paintings would be hung in the depots to invite people to get on board. That was in the early days of marketing. This was especially true for the Pacific Northwest region of the United States. As the facilities manager, I saw these paintings daily. Most of them were a pain to house, hang, or protect throughout the campus. On occasion, we would have tours of the campus, when people would stand in wonder of the paintings, or of the railcars that we had converted for meetings and/or dining, and of the architecture that we worked with every day. I had lost the wonder of what was in front of me. It took other people to remind me of the splendor of the provision.

Hillsong United recently released a song called "Wonder" that has transfixed me. There is a lyric describing God as the Wonder:

> And I'm walking in the light.
> I'm walking in the wonder.
> You're the wonder in the wild,
> Turning wilderness to wonder.

Part of repair is about seeing His wonder and seeing Him *as* wonder, as well as repairing your soul and reconnecting with God in ways that ministry has suffocated. It is important to finding that raw relational connection with God that steps out of processes and paperwork and leads back to the way we humans were designed.

SELF-CARE

Let's talk a little bit about self-care, because it's super important in the repair phase. First, what is self-care? The term has been used, and likely overused, in the last few years to the point that people don't really know what it means, or they simply apply their own meaning to it. So, let me clarify. Self-care is not a selfish goal to serve ourselves and meet our fleshly desires. Self-care is the process of being in tune with the God-designed needs of your body and mind and making sure you are intentionally living so that those God-designed needs are being valued and met as best they can be. I understand we can still have a debate about what those needs are, but here are a couple that I think are critical to understand.

Sleep
Your body is designed to need sleep. I have a neurologist (that's another story), and from the time I first saw him to the time we met back up several years later, he had converted his neurology office to a sleep and neurology lab. That happened because he found that most of the neurological things that his clients dealt with were caused by and resolved by sleep. Sleep is important. The brain goes through a detox process when it gets some sleep. A study of mice by Dr. Maiken Nedergaard and her colleagues at the University of Rochester Medical Center shows that the brain matter reduces in size during sleep to increase the space between gray matter, thereby allowing the cerebrospinal fluid to flow more easily and remove toxic matter.[1] Research the glymphatic system for more information on this. We truly do feel better mentally, for physiological reasons, when we get sleep. Additionally, a further

assumption, which is the foundation for EMDR therapy, is that when our body enters REM sleep stages, the eye movement we experience is part of a bilateral stimulation process that allows our neural networks to actively process thoughts, especially traumatic thoughts. This bilateral stimulation causes the brain to put events into the adaptive parts of the brain, minimizing the chances they will have lasting effects on our future relationships and efforts. Additionally, synaptic homeostasis is the process whereby our synapses between neurons shrink by as much as 20 percent to give our brains a rest so that they don't get overloaded. We are designed to rest!

There is so much to learn about the purpose and importance of sleep, but those are a few facts I like to share with clients to get them on board with the function and importance of sleep, even if they do think they can get by without it. Your body can't. Repair is a time to set new routines and to value what matters to your body so that it can operate in the way God designed it to operate. When I was younger, I collected articles and facts on the value of naps. I wish I could tell you why they fascinated me. Perhaps it's because my dad would often be found fast asleep in the rocking chair with a book on his lap, just for fifteen to thirty minutes. My mom would lie on her bed after getting back from church and nap in the afternoon with sun coming through the window. I enjoy a good nap as well. Unfortunately, the drive of progress and productivity has mostly robbed me of the luxury, but I am reconnecting with my old friend. There's a lot to be said for naps if you are a napper. My wife is not a napper—it messes up her sleep—but she's a sleeper, so that's OK. She's not me. Your body needs sleep. All bodies need sleep.

I have recently finished the book *Why We Sleep: Unlocking the Power of Sleep and Dreams* by Matthew Walker. I would highly encourage it as a staple for your self-care journey. Because of Walker's book and other research, I am comfortable saying that what happens to our brains while we sleep is more important than what happens to our brains while we are awake. Sleep is not a luxury but rather a misunderstood and highly neglected necessity for our mental health and our physical health.

Boundaries

One of the most important lessons to be taught is the value of boundaries. People need boundaries, but people don't have them. Drs. Cloud and Townsend have helped millions with their best-selling book by the same name and other versions written to address specific relationships and demographics. We need boundaries in order to live healthy lives. As mentioned in their book *Boundaries,*[2] you are your most valuable asset, and you are called to be a good steward of the assets God has given you. We think about our finances and our talents, but for some reason we miss the fact that we are responsible for how we treat, manage, and invest in ourselves. Boundaries help us do this.

Unfortunately, church is one of the worst places when it comes to respecting boundaries. We have this mindset that if we are doing ministry, it's OK, regardless of how much damage it is doing to our body, our families, or our marriages. On March 31, 2019, Pastor Pete Briscoe, senior pastor of Bent Tree Bible Church in Dallas, Texas, resigned after twenty-eight years.[3] In his departing message to the congregation, with his wife by his side, he shared publicly that he greatly had abandoned his wife during this journey. With tears in his eyes, he publicly said how much he appreciated her faithfulness throughout the years. It's not the first time this story has been told. It's not God's intention that a pastor husband should neglect his wife. In the same way as we neglect our spouses, we pastors push congregation members to serve, commit, join, be, do, and give. Then we wonder why our back door is so open. Not once do we teach a boundaries class because of fear that, rather than seeing us value our family members, colleagues, and congregants as God's creation and an asset, we would be creating a culture where everyone says *no* and our children's ministry would never be adequately staffed with volunteers. Repair is a good time to learn about boundaries. Of course, I'm not just talking about churches without boundaries. Boundarylessness mainly shows up in family dynamics as we try to manage guilt, shame, expectations, and our inability to say no or push back at all. Read the book, take a class (probably not at your church), and learn more about boundaries. I had a staff member once tell me, "If you think you're the only way God can accomplish what He wants to accomplish, that's pretty prideful." She was right.

GUILT, SHAME, INADEQUACY

I put these three things together because it's how I discuss them in my sessions with clients and because they are all related. There's also good chance you are dealing with these right now if you have picked up *Scream without Raising Your Voice*. And it's likely shame that is taking a front seat in your life. You may be thinking, *Something is wrong with me*. That's the difference between shame and guilt. Guilt simply says, *I've done something wrong*, and is a helpful moral compass. Shame, on the other hand, doesn't say to you that you have done something wrong but rather that you *are* wrong, that something is bad about you or wrong with you. It creates in us a sense of worthlessness. I like to break that down for my clients. Most of us with a decent knowledge of scripture will readily say we know we are not worthless, so I break it down by breaking the word in half. I ask, "Do you feel worth *less?*" Then I get the nods. Shame is Satan's powerful tool. If there were a competition for the most powerful tool in Satan's arsenal, I would certainly put shame in the running. When we repair, it is necessary that we deal with our shame.

Let's take a few minutes and walk through a helpful discussion that hopefully gives you some relief:

When we look at guilt, it's important that we understand that there is *true* guilt and *false* guilt. True guilt says that we have done something wrong or something against *our* moral and ethical compass that we have defined for ourselves. This compass is a productive tool we use to know that we have made a misstep or veered off from what we expected or wanted. It allows us to make adjustments, ask for forgiveness, and get back on track. False guilt, on the other hand, is a communication that we have done something wrong based on someone else's compass of expectations for either us or them. When your mom tells you that you should call her daily or be married by now, you may have a sense of false guilt. This feeling comes on also when the parents of the teens in your ministry tell you that you should have more activities, or the old people in your congregations tell you that the worship service needs more hymns. This is false guilt, founded on others' expectations. The challenge is that when you try to rectify false guilt, it can create true guilt, making you a people-pleaser, but very incongruent, and a person denying your own convictions. The additional challenge with false guilt is that if we suffer enough from it over the years, whether it be in our house growing up or in our Father's house as ministers, we begin to experience shame because false guilt grows shame. Why else would you continually think, do, and feel different from what other people think you should? There must be something wrong with you!

The antidote for this—and I think this is one of the most critical things to learn in ministry—is that you have to understand what your compass is. You have to know what *true* is for you so that you don't get compared to *false*. And hear me when I say that as you answer the question of what is true for you, you must not simply mention the Bible, which typically is not the area of contention, although it can be. What is true is what you have decided about what kind of person you want to be, what your schedule is, and how you do ministry. This is you knowing who you are and having an identity that you are OK walking in so that you can be comfortable with your compass. Anything else that is put upon you is considered as an opportunity for input or growth and then is either absorbed or rejected. There is no place in ministry for false guilt. Your true guilt lets you know that you have veered off course of being who you want to be, allowing you to adjust. Guilt is positive when managed appropriately.

Let me again suggest a book for you on shame that is, in my mind, a staple for your library, *Soul of Shame*,[4] by Curt Thompson. Dr. Thompson is a psychiatrist and deacon in Maryland. I'll borrow his joke by saying that there are plenty of clients for him in the DC area. <Awkward laughter in the audience.> If you deal with shame, I would encourage you to read *Soul of Shame* as part of your repair process, but I will share the punch line with you here. There is an antidote for shame, and it's healthy community. Genesis 2:18 says that it is not good for a human being to be alone, and a healthy community healing shame is just one of the many reasons that's true. Thompson shares that when we find ourselves in a safe community (for many of us, this doesn't yet exist), we can share our shame into the listening ears of safe recipients. In doing so, not only do we tame our shame, but also we let other people know that the space, whatever that may be in your case, is also safe for sharing those things that have kept them in bondage for possibly years. It's a healing process, and the antidote is us. This is one of the reasons that pastors suffer so badly. They feel they are at risk with their congregation, their church, their job, and their livelihood, and they cannot share their shame. So, it eats at them daily.

How do you know if you deal with shame? The best answer is that you do. But one thing you can look at to determine if you carry shame are what we call shame binds. A shame bind is an agreement you have made with yourself that you may or may not even realize. They all start with the words or thought "I don't deserve …." They can be picked up through trauma or simply from the comments of family friends or acquaintances. For instance, writing *Scream without Raising Your Voice* has been a chore for me. I don't type well, and as I age my typing ability seems to be getting worse. I may tell myself that no one wants to hear what I have to say (and maybe you don't), that I don't deserve having a book published, and so on and so on. If you don't like having a birthday celebration, it may be possible that you actually don't feel that you deserve to be celebrated. Don't deserve to have a big church? Don't deserve to have that position? Don't deserve to have your father's love? The list goes on. In high school, I was told by my math teacher that I was wasting my brain. I think he meant it in a positive way, but it still stung. I don't deserve the things that smart people have because I'm not using my brain wisely. Really?

Maybe this is difficult for you to see in yourself, or maybe it's difficult to admit. Get some professional help and deal with it as you repair. I also want to let you know that this is going to be an epidemic soon. In my opinion, Satan is advancing. If you walk through the average school nowadays, you'll see that our teachers are strapped and at their wits' end. We (the system) are backing them into proverbial (and sometimes actual) corners. They are tired and overwhelmed, and as a result, many times I hear the teachers resorting to shame-based motivation. It doesn't work. It destroys souls and creates a very burdened human. The same goes for parenting and marriage. We are getting lazy, tired, and frustrated as we resort to snide comments that say to us, *You are not worthy.* And we believe it.

Now let's talk about inadequacy. Such a negative word. Or is it? The truth is, although we believe that *inadequacy* is a negative word, it's really a positive word reminding us again that we need others. We are made to be communal; we are built to rely on and relate with others. The opposite of *inadequate* is *omnipotent*—and I'm pretty sure you wouldn't say that you are omnipotent, yet many people live with the burden to be so. As soon as we admit that we are inadequate, we can breathe easier, knowing that it's

OK to ask for help, refer that client, seek wisdom, say "I don't know," and be OK with who we are. Again, if we live with the mindset of omnipotence as normal, our inadequacy will funnel us into shame because, after all, what's wrong with us if others can and we can't?

UNLEARNING

The things we believe are amazing to me. In a recent audiobook, a concept was solidified for me. It was the concept that healthy development is about learning things for the first half of your life and then going through a process of unlearning. Think about that. Things are shared with us as we grow, and the learning institutions share things with us as we build our repertoire of knowledge. I think it's easy to grasp that. But the reality of it is that not everything we learn is accurate or healthy. Not every habit, "fact," or behavior is healthy for us. Some of these things are not even accurate. At some point it's important to put off childish things. Whether it's the definition of success, the way you handle your emotions, or the way you regard who Christ is or what He expects of you and has for you, you must look for the truth—and that truth may be that you must unlearn or, as some say, relearn. Unfortunately, many people don't take the time to unlearn, and their trajectory is stagnated maturity and minor growth. These are the people who still behave as they did in high school, still use the same coping mechanisms, and still watch WWF and think it's real. (I hope my junior high girlfriend reads this and has come to understand that there's some production going on there.) It really is hard to unlearn. We feel as if we've been duped, that we've wasted time, that we've been lied to, or that we are not very smart. It takes work to change, and let's face it, we're tired now and changing is a lot harder than becoming. It challenges our trust issues and can compromise our willingness to learn in the future if we admit that not all knowledge is accurate and healthy. But that is what maturity looks like. We must come to terms with this.

My father-in-law is a retired construction guy. In most of his later active years, he was a small general contractor who often did remodels and some new additions on a smaller scale. When I would work with him, I was often reminded that a remodel is so much harder to handle because you are required to work with what someone else has done before you, whether it was right or wrong. This is especially true when you must keep the system or the family working while you make the modifications. Keep using the bad way while building the new way. It's like the highway construction guys (I'm sure there's a real name for them, not "highway construction guys"), but how much easier is the first part of a highway's life—grading, framing, erecting, pouring—than the second or subsequent stages of its life when it's in operation and it needs to be modified? The system is at work around it, and we are not "allowed" to stop the productivity of life. Those guys are my heroes, even if I don't know what they are really called. Wait—civil engineers. There we go. As I get older, sometimes my brain decides on its own to unlearn stuff.

I won't go into the difficulties of change—there are many books and perspectives on that—but I will say that part of the repair process is the process of unlearning. For a more extended view on this, I refer to a book called *Transitions* written by Dr. William Bridges in 1991. He coined the Transition Model, which details the process of ending, hanging out in the neutral zone longer than one wants, and then making new beginnings.[5] For most of us, repair will require a separation, unlearning, and a temporary "un-identity" so that we can be renewed.

Scripture requires the same of us.

> When I was a child, I spake as a child, I understood as a child, I thought as a child: but when I became

a man, I put away childish things. (1 Corinthians 13:11)

Therefore if any man be in Christ, he is a new creature: old things are passed away; behold, all things are become new. (2 Corinthians 5:17)

What if you still believed in Santa Claus? What if you still thought throwing a temper tantrum in the grocery store was how to get something you wanted? What if ... oh, wait, that second one brought a name to your mind, didn't it?

Unlearning happens through perspective, feedback, and humility. We all have our bubbles in which we grow, and as we learn, we assume that living in our bubbles is the way of life. Most of my clients start a family-of-origin discussion with the statement "My family was pretty normal," and then they go into horrific or at least not-OK behaviors. Until you get out of your perspective bubble and get unbiased feedback from someone, you don't know that what you learned needs to be unlearned. The only perfect and unblemished curriculum is the Word of God, and even that is subject to misleading, abuse, and wrongful teaching. We need to be willing to unlearn. God will guide us in this if we ask. From perspectives of who *we* are to who God is, it is considered by some that our midlife crisis is really a coming to awareness that our facts are flawed and that our plans may not be achievable. We find we can't be anything we want to be and that our parents and teachers lied to us and thereby created shame because, if what they said is true, then we are not worthy, and we let not only those people but also ourselves down.

If we as pastors and ministry leaders don't get out of our bubbles and get other perspectives, if we don't seek feedback, if we aren't willing to admit previous errors of judgment or missteps, we will be stuck in our low trajectory of growth and be much less useful to God. Additionally, as we try to move on, our lack of unlearning will bring us back to the same patterns, systems, and rituals that got us to the place in which we found ourselves previously. As I like to say, "If nothing changes, nothing changes."

NOTHING

Speaking of nothing, I was motivated by the movie *Christopher Robin* to consider the importance of doing nothing. It was a pretty safe movie to watch on my bachelor weekend while I wrote and rested. It's a brilliantly simple movie about the beloved small-minded bear and his whimsical friends in the Hundred Acre Wood. I can't say that as a child I was much of a Winnie-the-Pooh fan, but I am now. Christopher Robin returns years later as an adult and, like many of us today, he needs to be reminded that the greatest somethings come out of doing nothing. There must be time for play and reflection as well as time for our bodies to calibrate and repair, for us to reconnect with others and ourselves, and for us to stop and hear what God wants us to hear. Rest is a critical piece of the cycle of life, but many ministry roles push us right through that cycle as we prepare, present, and push on day after day. Be honest. Ask yourself, "When was the last time I played?" I think this question is getting a little more publicity in the lives of ministry workers, but it's the secular world that is paying more attention. The World Health Organization is including burnout in the eleventh revision of the International Classification of Diseases (ICD-11). Burnout is defined as a syndrome conceptualized as resulting from chronic workplace stress that has not been successfully managed. I'm not saying burnout is directly linked to the absence of resting and playing, but I am saying that I suspect there's a significant correlation. In the *Ransomed Heart* podcast[6] of June 2019, the team discusses the importance of play in one's life, especially in ministry. I was triggered by their conversation of a smashball game frequently breaking out at some point in the workday. This same thing took place in my previous church. The millennials broke out the smashball set, but it was very difficult for me to engage because of my need for productivity, approval, and progress on the chores I had been assigned or had taken on. Work hard, get approval. We are wired and groomed based on our life stories, upbringings, and wounds to perceive things in certain ways. I hope *Scream without Raising Your Voice* is part of that renewing of your mind and learning what you need to unlearn. Hopefully, it will help you to see things a little differently if you have had a hard time with play. I engage in play so much better now in my new identity than when I was wandering in my no-man's-land. This is another reason that un-identity is an important part of the journey.

PLAYFULNESS

Speaking of play, one of my favorite parts of repair is seeing God as playful again. I enjoy looking at Him as a loving Father who enjoys meeting me in unique ways. But when one is in survival mode, that part of the relationship is often hard to foster. However, if you can gain some ground and find some focus on this, you will find that He is oh-so-playful and loves to add levity. One of my favorite stories of His playfulness in my life takes place when I was at a conference in Colorado Springs. It had been a rough season, and I was looking for restoration of my soul as the conference promised. As I made my way down the hall of the church building that was hosting the event, I remember specifically asking that I see God's hand in this. The specific wording is important. But I didn't yet realize how important it was.

There on the floor, just lying there, was a playful thing for me to discover. It was the hand of one of those poseable Jesus action figures. OK, fine, it was a Jesus doll—not a hand *on* the doll that I noticed, just *the* hand. It was the hand of God. I hope you're laughing. Not only is this playful, but also it's uniquely special to me because I happen to have a hand collection (another story in itself) that now includes a very small and special hand of God. God is playful.

CHAPTER 9

RECALIBRATE

Healing from unhealthy relationships doesn't just require repair. At some point, it requires recalibrating your sense of who you are. In trauma, things happen—beliefs get established, and things get said and felt that, without an honest look at who you are and were, will likely cause you to fall back into those same systemic issues in your next season. Like crawling off a battlefield, shell-shocked and bewildered, taking an honest look at where you might have misunderstood yourself or pretended to be someone else is something you need to do. Again, thinking of the battered spouse, some of your basic truths of value and ability need to be reestablished. Negative belief patterns need to be denied, and the true you needs to have permission to come back out into the world. And it's not as easy as you think.

IDENTITY

I recently spent a season becoming someone I was not designed to be. Before you think this is going to be deep and spiritual, let me just say that I'm talking about my hair. I like long hair. I like the way it looks, the way it gives a sense of youthfulness and artistic effort. I like full beards, trimmed into a neat and healthy shape, again giving the look of artistic prowess and virility. There's something edgy about a guy with a full beard, and there's something young and professional about a manicured mane. So that's how the journey began. Besides, my wife likes long hair. The only issue was that I had short hair. But hair grows, so I thought, *Let's do this.* I'm not a fast beard grower, but progress was made, and the hair came along nicely. The problem was that my hair didn't exactly look like that young artistic hair. It looked like old, wavy, awkward hair. My hairdresser kept making the promise that more length would weigh it down. Yet the longer it got, the less it cooperated. Now with weight comes thickness for some of us, and man, was thick getting to me. The beard required product, and the hair required product. It didn't look like it was me in the mirror anymore, and to be honest, I wasn't happy trying to be who I thought I wanted to be. Other people liked it. I didn't. One day, I woke up and said, "I'm done. I'm through pretending to be someone else. I need to get back to who I really am." A number-two guard on a trimmer ran across my whole head. I had a little fun with a new hairdresser when I fabricated a startled look as the first locks fell.

It felt amazing, not just from the physical relief but also from the psychological reality that this was who I was designed to be—short hair, goatee, and that's all. I tell this story because many times, in and out of ministry, we get wrapped up in who John Eldredge would call "The Poser."[7] There is an incongruence between who we are and who we are meant to be. Sometimes this is trauma induced; sometimes this is by choice. There's a disconnect between who we want to be, who others want us to be, who God wants us to be, and who the world sees us as. In ministry, we pastors often end up assuming the role that the congregation puts on us rather than staying true to the calling God has given us. Or maybe it's a role the elders have assumed and foisted upon us that is not true when measured against what God is nudging us to be on the inside. Maybe you have become who you are to protect yourself against unhealthy behavior and relationships, or maybe you are responding to false guilt. Living this way is tiresome and frustrating; it isn't what God had in mind.

To recalibrate is to realign yourself with your identity in God. The challenging part is that in the transition, we often step out of a false identity into no identity because the false identity was the only identity we had. Or maybe it wasn't the only identity, but it was the identity that we used in order to get our needs met. It was our mechanism for approval or affirmation. Maybe it was our mechanism for comfort or appreciation. Stepping away from that false identity may be one of the hardest things you do in your lifetime because on the other side is temporarily no identity with no needs being met. Talk about lonely. You have just entered the desert.

But be patient. It will come. Ask God to reveal to you your true identity in Him and His plans for you—you know, the ones that the scriptures tell us about in Ephesians 2:10:

> For we are his workmanship, created in Christ Jesus unto good works, which God hath before ordained that we should walk in them.

This is a good reminder that you aren't out there wandering in the desert alone with purposelessness; He knew you before you were born, and He has plans for you. You have an identity and a purpose. Ask Him and He will reveal it to you. It's hard to resist the desire to make our own identity, but He will help us to rest in who He has made us to be.

You're probably asking how to do this right about now. I wish I had all the answers. I don't. But I do have some thoughts. It starts by being authentic. I recently presented to a group of pastors on identity and made use of the Johari window. Heard of it? It's a good way to get back to who we are—shave the beard, drop the façade, and be authentic. Let me explain. The Johari window[8] is a technique or diagram that helps people better understand their relationship with others and themselves. It was created in 1955 by psychologists Joseph Luft (1916–2014) and Harrington Ingham (1916–1995). It looks like this:

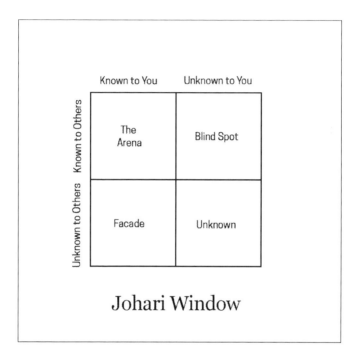

There are four areas to be aware of as we look at a person or ourselves, as follows:

Johari Window Area 1 - the Arena
This is the area that is known to others and yourself. I am a man. I have a wife. I am losing my hair. I have mood swings and other things that are obvious or that I have shared.

Johari Window Area 2 – the Façade
This area consists of things that are known to you but that you haven't shared with others. They are the façade you hide

behind. I could tell you of a few, but that would put them in the other category. Just trust me when I say that I haven't told you everything. Likewise, you have secrets. Maybe you fear failure. Maybe you're insecure in a crowd. Maybe you hate the way you look or you hate the sound of your voice. Façades appear here as we hide these things from others, for example, I know I'm scared, but you think I'm confident.

These next two are areas you *don't* know about yourself, but these are the *fact* of who you *are*.

Johari Window Area 3 - Blind Spots

Other people know it, but you don't. The first thing that comes to mind is negatives. It could be that you don't read social cues well and, thus, you make conversations awkward. Or it might be that you come across as arrogant. Or maybe you have a fear-based living style or a mindset of scarcity that has never been acknowledged. But sometimes positives lie in this area as well. You could be good with empathy and administration, or there could be a potential in you that you don't see but others do. It's your blind spot.

Johari Window Area 4 - the Unknown

In this area are things that *are you*, but neither you nor others see them. It's the unknown. This one can be kind of scary until you realize that God, who made you, knows what's in *all* the squares. So, I guess, technically, this area doesn't really exist.

But for the sake of the Johari window exercise, I will say that the power of area 4 is not only in the things we haven't identified but also in the lies that we don't realize we live with that others and we ourselves believe. Both are wrong. These aren't facades. In my world, these are subconscious responses to repressed memories, wounds, and shame that silently eat at us and affect our behavior and frame of mind.

Think about the square and how it relates to your life. What do you and other people know to be true? What do you know to be true but haven't revealed to others? What are you unaware of about yourself that others know to be true? What is true about you but you have not identified it? In a *Desiring God* article,[9] I read the following quote: "Our identity is for the sake of making known His identity." Now think about your square. Paul Tripp, when talking about identity in his book *Dangerous Calling*, uses the metaphor of carnival mirrors.[10] As we receive our identity from others, it distorts us; it's not the fact of who we are. Of course, that metaphor took my brain to James 1:23–24:

> For if any be a hearer of the word, and not a doer,
> he is like unto a man beholding his natural face
> in a glass: For he beholdeth himself, and goeth
> his way, and straightway forgetteth what manner
> of man he was.

So, as we think about the question "Are we finding our identity in Him?" I think it's best answered by asking if His identity is found in us.

So, who *are* you? If we look at the rescue and the repair, maybe it's worth asking who you *were*. Was your ministry defining you? That's idolatry. Were others defining you? That's codependency. Are your ailments and shortcomings defining you? That borders on blasphemy. Is God's image defining you? That's holy. That's worship. That's your identity. Let's go back to the window.

The goal is not to move everything to one big gigantic fully known square where your dirty laundry is hanging there for everyone to see. Even Jesus went away to lonely places to have conversations with His Father. He told the disciples things when He felt it was appropriate to tell them. They didn't know everything about Jesus.

The goal is for your authentic self to come out from behind lies.

This allows your gifts to be acknowledged and your shortcomings to be given to God, thus allowing Him to change them if He wants. So, your squares may end up looking more like this:

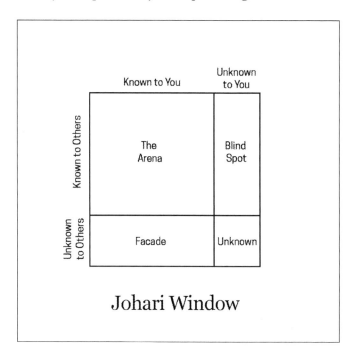

As we think about identity, I encourage you to start by seeing how you can safely make area 1 bigger and have the others shrink. Let's take a quick look at how you can do that.

Area 1: Know that just because it's in the "everybody knows it" box doesn't mean it's good. There's "bad" stuff in area 1 for sure. Remember vulnerability? It helps in three ways: (1) It feels better for you because you're no longer hiding your identity. No more lies and cover-ups. (2) It helps the issue get addressed. God can use your community to address it if He wants it to be addressed. (3) Ultimately, it allows people to see God's image and mercies in you as you grow and deal with your stuff. Bringing it into the light, dealing with it, and being authentic in who you are is the goal.

Area 2: This is where we practice vulnerability. Self-disclosure to safe people is freeing. Shame is overcome, and authenticity is reinforced. Not only does it free *you*, but also it frees up those with whom you share. Again, it's not a "dump your laundry" situation; it is moving into vulnerability with safe people, which is necessary. Again, I encourage you to read Curt Thompson's book *Soul of Shame* for a beautiful picture and much more articulate conversation on the topic. It has truly been life-changing for me and many others.

Area 3: Here you need to get feedback. What do people know about you that needs to be addressed? Maybe there are skill sets you haven't allowed God to use in you. There may even be character traits that you are blind to that keep hurting people or holding you back from your own success. This is probably the most powerful and concerning area to my mind, something about you that could be addressed but you haven't asked what it is. Or it may be that you're not willing to hear the answer. We all need feedback.

Area 4: This area has a lot of unknowns and is an opportunity for continual learning and exploration. Ask questions, take courses, get counseling, read, and be open. Again, community is critical. Ask God to reveal in you what needs to be revealed.

As you repair, it's important to ask, "Who am I?" It's three words. Likely you have a church answer, but it can be a very difficult question if you sit in it for a while and admit some truths about who you are. It can be difficult to be honest with yourself because who wants to admit they aren't where they want to be? But that's OK because we are now in a place from which we can move forward.

In Bridges's *Transitions*, he talks about this time between endings and beginnings as no-man's-land. It's necessary to go through this lonely and disconnected time to have a new beginning. Think about trying to be new while holding onto the old. It's not what is intended at all. To quote the theology of Winnie-the-Pooh, "I often get to where I'm going by walking away from where I've been." It's interesting how many of us *try* to get to where we're going by staying where we are.

Our ultimate goal here is for our identity to reflect His identity, and we do that by being who He wants us to be. As you come to better understand who He is, you come to better understand who you are. Repair is a time of coming to know Him better and coming to know yourself better.

FIVE S'S

Another tool worth considering is a diagram I created with a colleague of mine that we simply call the Five S's, something we use in working with men, but it's not gender-specific. It's about recalibrating, healing, unlearning, and doing self-assessment. Consider that you were created the way God designed you, nothing more, nothing less. You are effective for the tasks He has prepared for you. For my analogy, it's best to picture the hull of a boat, honed, smoothed, waxed, and beautiful for cutting through the water. You are that boat.

The Five "S's

IDENTITY

That hull is comprised of your unique personality traits and giftings that uniquely compose you so that you can do the things that God has designed you for. We have hundreds of these traits and giftings, uniquely us, but for the sake of the diagram and conversation, I usually just draw eight to ten character traits to get the point across. They are perfect in their original state, as I mentioned, honed and waxed. But as we grow and learn and exist in this broken world, we begin to collect barnacles on our boat. These barnacles are four of the five S's. Barnacles make us less effective, slow us down, and hinder us in our work. Let's look at each of the Five S's:

SOLIDS

The solids are who you are, the you God designed and created, wonderfully and fearfully made with a spirit of power, love, and self-discipline. We often forget who we are: made in God's image as heirs to the throne, children of God. We can go on and on and on. This is *solid* stuff. I would challenge you, if you are struggling, to go through this "on and on" and spend time fully understanding who you are in Christ and see what you come up with. Solids let you be effective. Your hull cuts through the challenges of life and makes it look easy. I picture the college athletes at the Harvard–Yale Regatta cutting through the water of the mist-covered Thames river. They would never allow barnacles or abrasions to be on their boats. You are solid in how you were created. No blemishes, no mistakes.

Solids are *true* and *good* and need to be *kept* and *cultivated*.

SIN

Simply put, sin affects our effectiveness, and it must be addressed. I don't even think I have mentioned this directly in *Scream without Raising Your Voice* yet, but as we look at our role in the ministry dynamic or challenges of life, we need to determine where we have separated from God. What do we need to take credit for and ownership of? Sin muddies our perspective and hinders our relationships. It leads us back to maladaptive coping and isolates us further. The awesome part of this, however, is that sin can be dealt with. Or should I say it *has* been dealt with.

Sin is dealing with what is *true* and *bad*. It needs to be *exposed* and *expelled*.

STAINS

Throughout our lives, we will have things "happen" that are not true but that affect the perception of our character. Sometimes only others' perceptions of us are affected, but sometimes we believe those same stains exist. These can be criticisms or lies, or maybe a onetime mistake that garnished holistic application. Maybe it was guilt by association or just someone else's problem projected onto you. Stains come in all shapes and sizes and at all ages. They need to be addressed to clear up the way these barnacles steer you in the wrong or ineffective direction, thereby undermining your effectiveness.

Stains are *false* and *bad,* and they need to be *dissected* and *disowned.*

It's important to note that these need to be dissected because, if they *are* true, they now become sins and need to be handled as such.

SHAMS

Let's head back to poser mentality and realize that sometimes *we* put the barnacle on the boat. This is something that needs to be addressed. Shams represent when we are faking our talents and living unauthentically because we want to look good, we want to be thought highly of, or we are simply afraid of being who we are. We fake it, falsify it, and feel like someone we aren't. This may work for a while, but eventually it causes fatigue and mental breakdown because of this incongruence of self that we have been dealing with.

Shams are *false* and *"good"* (notice the quotation marks) and need to be *renounced* and *rejected.*

SHAMES

Shames are barnacles that others put on your hull to slow you down in order to help them win. These are often some of the biggest barnacles we deal with. A situation or characteristic of ours is taken and used against us to the detriment of our core beliefs of self. They are hard to separate from because they are us or they actually did happen. We did wet the bed, or forget the report, or get angry, or miss the easy goal. Or we are overweight or short or nerdy. These barnacles stick hard to the hull and can often take years to remove. Most of us just live with them. But as mentioned before, what can be hard or impossible to remove alone can come off through community. It's really the only way shame barnacles can be removed.

Shames are *true* and *shaming* (not good or bad in themselves—just facts) and need to be *shared* and *subdued*.

Here's a look at a person covered in the barnacles of life.

What do you need to scrub out of your life?

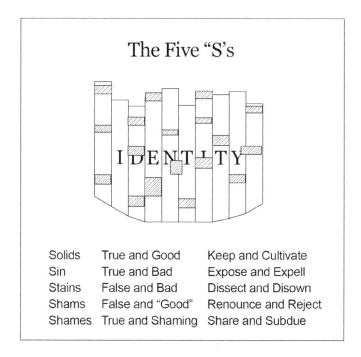

The Five "S's

I D E N T I T Y

Solids	True and Good	Keep and Cultivate
Sin	True and Bad	Expose and Expell
Stains	False and Bad	Dissect and Disown
Shams	False and "Good"	Renounce and Reject
Shames	True and Shaming	Share and Subdue

The Five S's are just a tool used to look at what has become of us and where we need to unlearn undesirable behaviors, refocus our attention, and reclaim what God has intended. It's not intended to cause shame; we are all equal in this. It's not intended to stain your life story; we all have one. It's simply a feedback process of seeing who we are and where, perhaps, we need to adjust for the next season of our lives.

Paul adjusted, Moses adjusted, and David adjusted. Saul did not. Recalibrating is about setting our broken bones, lifting with our legs, eating more fiber, getting the medicine, and doing things differently, in the way that we were truly designed to do them.

Times of conflict, unrest, pain, and confusion are times for assessing and reconnecting with God. While you wait on rescue, take a hard look at what is really going on in your life and where God may be leading you. What does this season expose in you and about your way of doing life? What patterns, urges, needs, and emotions have surfaced that need to be addressed? What has this time exposed in your surroundings and the environment you work in that's unhealthy for you? Be curious; ask God to show you. If you expose a material to high heat or extreme cold, you will find its weakness, either visually by seeing the thin broken cracks or physically by observing how it performs. The same is true for a system or a person. Your church may be in a time of stress, and you may be seeing how ineffective the weak communication style is or how the shallow prayer life responds. You may be in stress and see how weak your self-care program is or how shallow your relational connections are, both vertically and horizontally. Notice those things and make adjustments.

If you listen to any life coach or behavioral scientist worth his or her weight in salt (whatever that means), you will likely hear this person say that one of our biggest issues is that we live life by default. We let life happen, responding with our reflexes and acting by our habits. Paying attention to the world around you, noticing your thoughts and emotions, and choosing to be curious allows you to actively become who you want to become, or at least make strides in the direction toward, hopefully, who God wants you to become.

CHAPTER 10

REDEMPTION

I have a redeemer and it is not me.

—Dr. Matthew LaGrange

I have resisted writing this chapter, not just because it's chronologically last, but because I'm not there yet, and I'm concerned about what my words will be. As Dr. Bridges references in *Transitions*, I am in many ways in the neutral zone between endings and beginnings.[11] I have unlearned so many things.

Redemption is the act of "buying back" or "to buy out." I want to be clear: I am redeemed through Christ, and I am not seeking redemption again. It has been done. Once, forever. Just to provide clarity, I will use a capital *R* when speaking of the Redemption provided by Christ. The redemption in this chapter is a more nonspiritual use that is common in English vernacular to simply convey that what was not worthy is now worthy, or what was spent has now been shown to be worth what was received in exchange. "Was my story worth it?" and "Is your story worth it?" are the questions. Were my actions, my experiences, and my choices worth the energy, the years, and the relationships that were extended? We know that in the best stories, pain is used to create purpose, tragedy gets meaning, and ultimately that purpose and meaning is God's glory when Redemption is achieved.

> Jesus answered, "Neither hath this man sinned, nor his parents: but that the works of God should be made manifest in him." (John 9:3)

In John, there is the beautiful story of redemption regarding this man's handicap. The handicap was given purpose and meaning, and God's glory was seen through it. It wasn't wasted or worthless. The man wasn't worthless or even "worth less." He was able to glorify God because of his infirmity. That's what redemption looks like. When we see a definition like this, our tendency is to hope or expect that we will be part of some clear-cut moment of redemption. This is when everyone at the dinner party gets to hear the punch line and there is a big sigh of relief. Everyone gets to see how it all makes sense and why it was all worth it, and then they get to celebrate. I hope that works for you. And trust me, sometimes it does work. Sometimes, in hindsight, the story comes together and we get to say, "Wow, now I see what He was doing." Just like my message to those teens back in chapter 1 when I looked at "Here Comes the Boom!" But we sure don't need to live with this as an expectation. As we step into a faith situation of trusting God amid adversity, trauma, or confusion, a focus on a perceived redemptive plan in our minds can be a distraction to the fulfillment of the Redemptive plan in God's mind, His glory. We must continue in that faith walk, unsure of the details of our journey, while allowing the maturation of the redemptive process to occur.

I think about times when my kids asked me how to do something or where something was, and in the middle of my explaining the process or the location of an item, they thought they had an understanding of the whole process, so they took over the conversation or task and wildly missed the point. It's like buzzing into a *Family Feud* question too early and answering "Change their diapers" as a premature answer to the question "Name something that a mother does for her baby ..." before hearing "...that she also does for her husband." It's God's plan that has been started, and putting expectations on it will not serve us well. Thinking we know the answer and taking over will not normally allow us to win the round.

What we can know is that the Redemption happened for our lives when Christ died on the cross, and it is working itself out in our lives and in the world as you read and as we live. It will happen regardless of the size of our church or the size of the sins in our lives. It will happen whether we made a "right" choice or a "wrong" choice. I think sometimes we forget that. We forget that it's not about works, or meeting the goals our parents set for us, whether they were implicitly or expressly shared. It's not about the shame we carry, the mistakes we made, or how many people with whom we have shared the gospel. It really isn't. There are no metrics involved with Redemption except that Christ suffered and died for our sins and bought us out of death for His glory and to be united with Him. I know you know this, but there are so many things that I know that I enjoy reading or hearing again to let them sink in. And let's face it, sometimes we don't live as if we know it. Sometimes we don't lead a church as we know it. Redemption will happen for humanity. That's where our focus needs to be. Spoiler alert: that's the way the story ends. I love John Eldredge's reminder of this in his book *All Things New*, where he says that we are to focus on the restoration of life and on the new heaven and the new earth as it is to come. He suggests that we grab it with two hands and seize it, instead of holding on to our redemption, our to-do list, and our bucket list.[12]

So then, why did I title this last chapter "Redemption," and then go on to talk about Redemption, and then say redemption isn't something that we can expect or work toward? For me, honestly, it started as a need for meaning for my journey; I felt the need to know that I had done good things and made good choices. My need for approval and an acknowledgment of being obedient has no doubt tainted my thought process. My need to make redemption more important than Redemption is really where my mind was. But it has now become about hope—hope that the path that I laid out is the path that God has for me or, if it's not, hope that He will use my pain and any misinterpretations along the way for His glory regardless. I say that I feel comfortable that God provided the paths I chose, but in my being human, I have times of questioning if perhaps it was more about me—if somewhere my story got mixed up with His. Perhaps it was pride or even ignorance. Somehow, if redemption for my story comes, so too would clarity that I *did* do the right thing, and that my father *does* love me, and that it's all going to be OK. Getting redemption means I didn't mess up my wife's life and my kids' lives, or the lives of anyone else I influenced along the way. I type that out here so that both you and I can see how flawed this thinking is. I type it out so you can see how my need for redemption of my story likely ties back to my need for acceptance and approval in my childhood and my need to have done the right thing. I don't do the wrong things well. I wonder if maybe you have this need as well. Maybe we share this need for redemption to stave off another infusion of shame, another attack of disappointment, and fear of failure.

Here's the reality: I do pray that my story will be redeemed, and I pray that many others' stories will be also. I admit it's a selfish, misguided, prayer, but I'm honest with God, and I encourage you to be as well. What I am working on is being OK with God's using my story regardless of my comfort or my expectation of His glory. I'm working on knowing that any pride, misinterpretations, or failures do not preclude God from using me for His glory, regardless of my redemption. Somewhere I have in my head that I want to be used as a good example and not a bad example. That itself is pride. If God is the purpose, then He can use me in either format. That's what I'm working on. I'm praying that lessons learned and conversations had along the way will be used to strengthen His church and His kingdom. I pray that others have grown and that I continue to do so as well. But mostly I pray that redemption comes to glorify God, regardless of my outcome. Easy to write, but hard to live. Actually, it was hard to write too. And before you comfort me and let me know it's all going to be OK, know that there are many well-meaning Christians who stir up this pot daily by misusing verses such as Jeremiah 29:11 all the time:

> For I know the thoughts that I think toward you, saith the Lord, thoughts of peace, and not of evil, to give you an expected end.

Or Romans 8:28:

> And we know that all things work together for good to them that love God, to them who are the called according to his purpose.

"Don't worry, everything's going to be OK." However, we see clearly through the stoning of Steven, and the crucifying of Peter, and the beheading of John (and the list goes on up to modern times) that these verses don't mean what such folks who say such things think they do. I know that the reality is that "bad" things might happen and that things may not go the way I (note that word *I*) want them to. The redemption may not play out the way I hoped it would. That's what I'm working on. The truth is that the *only redemption we can truly count on for sure is the Redemption that Christ has provided* and will provide when the earth is made new and love wins. This is a guarantee.

Also know that being on a journey for redemption of the past may be a distraction from the story God has for you and may be more about your personal needs than about God's will and His desire for you. I do pray that redemption comes for you if that's where you are, and that it comes in the way you imagined, but that's not the goal. I'm reminded of James 4:15, which reads:

> For that ye ought to say, If the Lord will, we shall live, and do this, or that.

I pray that if it is the Lord's will for redemption to come to your story, you indeed get to see it happen. My greater hope and prayer for you is that you find God and His hope through and within this journey—not as a journey to some desired redemption to make your pain worth it but as a journey into Him that has a very unpredictable path but a constant purpose. If you are in a place where you feel that you need redemption, I would direct you in two ways.

First of all, leaning into your story and finding God through any efforts and interpretations can bear amazing fruit. Being obedient in faith, being a faithful boot camp recruit, will produce change. Persevering through our dark nights of the soul will grow us and reintroduce us to Him in powerful ways. We do have a role, but it's not to obtain redemption for ourselves; it's to do what we are always called to do, and that is to live the gospel, seek God, and trust in His will for us. Even more so in our times of transition and confusion, we're to call out to Him and seek His guidance.

Secondly, when we look at that desired redemption, we need to see that the manifestation of it is often incremental and, in some cases, downright scary and/or uncomfortable. We need to understand that if redemption is currently available to us, more often than not we will find it in little things and the little lessons. It most likely won't be in dinner party format but rather small personal moments of awareness and realization. I wonder if, perhaps, those who don't feel that they find redemption in their stories have failed to pay attention to the small changes in search of the bigger moments, or if they have focused on *their* expectation of redemption instead of seeing what God is doing along the way. If I set my sights, which I have, on a successful business of restorative care for pastors being *the* redemption that would make it all worthwhile, then there is a chance that it will not occur, and then I may find myself not understanding why I went through everything, why God had forsaken me, so to speak—which I know isn't true. If I am never able to lay out a grand plan in retrospect as to how my story was redeemed, then life can be shameful and disappointing. But if I can look at daily or weekly areas of growth in my life as part of His redemptive plan, then I can be content. If I know that unlearning a behavior, or widening a bias, or suffering, or finding joy like I've never had before is all part of His redemptive plan to make me better for Him, then I have put *myself* in the correct place in the equation.

Whether you are looking at *Scream without Raising Your Voice* from the future, present, or past perspective, it's critical that you remind yourself that Redemption *will* arrive, and it will be as God designed and declared. It will happen in His timing. There is no boss, congregation, elder, or parent who can stop it from happening. Your screams need to be directed to God to give you clarity and direction in managing your situations and preparing for them. Send your confusion and pain to Him. Seek to serve Him and separate yourself, as best you can, from your fears of misalignment, misinterpretation, and failure. You cannot thwart Redemption.

It's redemption enough to know that He is working on me for Himself, regardless of me, regardless of my expectations. Regardless of our relational needs or our past, redemption comes when we, through our stories, come to love and validate Him regardless of our circumstances or challenges. Our redemption comes when we see the changes He is making in us, for Him.

NOTES

Past

1   S. Achor, *Before Happiness: The 5 Hidden Keys to Achieving Success, Spreading Happiness, and Sustaining Positive Change* (New York: Crown, 2013).

2   J. Eldredge, *Wild at Heart: Discovering the Secret of a Man's Soul* (Nashville: Thomas Nelson, 2011).

3   D. Ferguson, *Top Ten Relational Needs* (Cedar Park, TX: Intimacy Press, 2007).

4   J. Eldredge, *Walking with God: How to Hear His Voice* (Nashville: Nelson Books, 2016).

Present

1   R. Rohr, *True Self, False Self—the Divine Indwelling: Bearing the Burden* (Cincinnati: Franciscan Media, 2013).

2   A. P. Boers, "Everyone's Pastor, No One's Friend," *Christianity Today,* Winter 1991, https://www.christianitytoday.com/pastors/1991/winter/91l1130.html.

3   B. van der Kolk, M.D., *The Body Keeps the Score: Mind, Brain, and Body in the Transformation of Trauma* (New York: Penguin, 2015).

4   S. Eldredge, *You Are Captivating: Celebrating a Mother's Heart* (Nashville: Thomas Nelson, 2014).

5   C. G. Jung, *Memories, Dreams, Reflections* (New York: Random House, 1963).

6   Holt-Lunstad, Smith, and Layton, "Social Relationships and Mortality Risk: A Meta-Analytic Review," *PLOS Medicine*, July 27, 2010, https://doi.org/10.1371/journal.pmed.1000316.

7   C. Thompson, *The Soul of Shame: Retelling the Stories We Believe about Ourselves* (Downers Grove, IL: InterVarsityPress, 2015).

8   S. R. Covey, *The 7 Habits of Highly Effective People—Powerful Lessons in Personal Change: Restoring the Character Ethic* (New York: Free Press, 2004).

9   E. Briceño, "How to Get Better at the Things You Care About," filmed November 2016 at TEDxManhattanBeach, TED video, 11:14, https://www.ted.com/talks/eduardo_briceno_how_to_get_better_at_the_things_you_care_about?language=en.

10 P. Hiett, "The Abundance of Shared Poverty," YouTube April 11, 2010, video, https://www.youtube.com/watch?v=QDyzz7tJq8Y.

11 P. Shirer, *Awaken: 90 Days with the God Who Speaks* (Nashville: B&H Publishing Group, 2017.

12 K. Westcott, "What Is Stockholm Syndrome?" *BBC News*, August 22, 2013, https://www.bbc.com/news/magazine-22447726.

13 C. Dickens (1859). *A Tale of Two Cities*. London: Chapman & Hall.

14 J. B. Rotter, "Generalized Expectancies for Internal versus External Control of Reinforcement," *Psychological Monographs: General and Applied* 80, no. 1 (1966): 1-128. https://doi:10.1037/h0092976.

Future

1   Lulu Xie, et al, "Sleep Drives Metabolite Clearance from the Adult Brain," *Science* 342, no. 6156 (October 18, 2013): 373. https://doi.org/10.1126/science.1241224.

2   H. Cloud, & J.S. Townsend, *Boundaries: When to Say Yes, How to Say No to Take Control of Your Life* (Grand Rapids, MI: Zondervan, 2017).

3   "Pete's Announcement" Accessed October 1, 2020. https://benttree.org/update-on-pete/

4   C. Thompson, *The Soul of Shame: Retelling the Stories We Believe about Ourselves* (Downers Grove, IL: InterVarsityPress, 2015).

5   W. Bridges, S. Bridges, *Transitions: Making Sense of Life's Changes* (New York: Lifelong Books, 2019).

6   "The Serious Business Of Play," Accessed January 4, 2020, https://wild@heart.org/rhplay/podcast/serious-business-play-0.

7   J. Eldredge, *Wild at Heart: Discovering the Secret of a Man's Soul* (Nashville: Thomas Nelson, 2011).

8   J. Luft, H. Ingham, "The Johari window, a graphic model of interpersonal awareness," *Proceedings of the Western Training Laboratory in Group Development*. University of California, Los Angeles (1955).

9   J. Piper, "Christian Identity and Christian Destiny," Desiring God, April 17, 1994, https://www.desiringGod.org/messages/christian-identity-and-christian-destiny.

10 P.D. Tripp, *Dangerous Calling: Confronting the Unique Challenges of Pastoral Ministry* (Wheaton, IL: Crossway, 2012).

11 W. Bridges, S. Bridges, *Transitions: Making Sense of Life's Changes* (New York: Lifelong Books, 2019).

12 J. Eldredge, *All Things New: Heaven, Earth, and the Restoration of Everything You Love* (Nashville: Nelson Books, 2018).

Printed in the United States
by Baker & Taylor Publisher Services